Alan Maxwell Boisragon

The Benin Massacre

Alan Maxwell Boisragon

The Benin Massacre

ISBN/EAN: 9783743414938

Manufactured in Europe, USA, Canada, Australia, Japa

Cover: Foto ©ninafisch / pixelio.de

Manufactured and distributed by brebook publishing software (www.brebook.com)

Alan Maxwell Boisragon

The Benin Massacre

THE

BENIN MASSACRE

BY

CAPTAIN ALAN BOISRAGON
ONE OF THE TWO SURVIVORS

COMMANDANT OF
THE NIGER COAST PROTECTORATE FORCE

WITH PORTRAIT AND SKETCH MAP

METHUEN & CO.
36 ESSEX STREET, W.C.
LONDON
1897

TO
E. M. B.

NOTE

IN the following account of our escape from that awful Benin Massacre, I have tried to keep away from all questions of politics and policy, and to give my own opinion as little as possible.

CONTENTS

CHAP.		PAGE
I.	HISTORY OF BENIN	1
II.	THE ROYAL NIGER COMPANY AND H.B.M.'S NIGER COAST PROTECTORATE	21
III.	POSITION OF BENIN	44
IV.	OUR EXPEDITION	53
V.	OUR EXPEDITION (*continued*)	71
VI.	OUR ESCAPE	90
VII.	OUR ESCAPE (*continued*)	112
VIII.	OUR ESCAPE (*continued*)	132
IX.	OUR ESCAPE (*continued*)	152
X.	THE PUNITIVE EXPEDITION	167

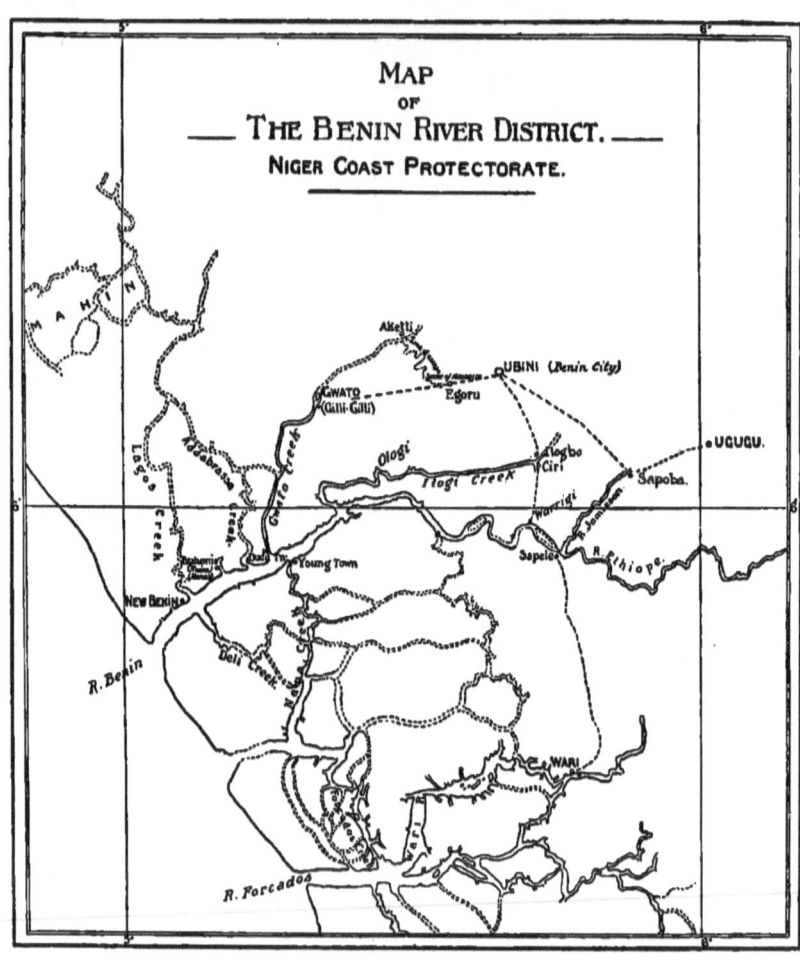

THE BENIN MASSACRE

CHAPTER I

HISTORY OF BENIN

BENIN seems to have been a kingdom from time immemorial, anyway from before its first discovery by the Portuguese, somewhere at the end of the fourteenth or beginning of the fifteenth century. By their discoveries, the Portuguese for a long time had all the benefits of the trade to be obtained from West Africa. They were followed some time after by the Dutch and Swedes. It was not till the year 1552 that the English began to visit these parts; and in 1588 Queen Elizabeth granted a charter to an African Company of English Merchants, who thereupon started trading all over the West Coast of Africa, much to the annoyance of the Dutch and Portuguese.

The first English expedition to visit Benin City started in two ships and a pinnace from Bristol in 1553, under the command of two captains, Windham and Antonio Anes Pinteado. The latter, as his name indicates, was a Portuguese, and seems to have been a most excellent man as well as a skilled navigator. At one time he was in such favour with the King of Portugal that he was appointed to take care of the Coasts of Brazil and Guinea against the French, " to whom," as his old biographer[1] says, " he was a terror in these seas." This expedition never promised to be much of a success, as from the very first Captain Windham seems to have been "a terror to" the worthy Pinteado, and treated him infamously through the whole voyage,—amongst other things, threatening to cut off the ears of "this rascally Jew," as he called him, and nail them to the mast. They seem to have been about six months in arriving

---

[1] One Richard Eden, who published a small collection of travels in 1577.

at the mouth of the Benin River, from whence they sent up the pinnace as near as they could get to Benin City. Here Captain Pinteado with an English gentleman called Nicholas Lambert and other merchants landed, and were conducted to the King's Court, ten leagues from the river. They seem to have had a most friendly reception from His Majesty, "a black moor or negro," who spoke to them in Portuguese, which he had learnt when a child. After discovering that they had come for purposes of trading, the King not only promised to fill their ships with pepper, which seems to have been the great article of trade at that time, but also, in case they had not enough merchandise to pay for the pepper, the King actually proposed to give them credit for it till next season, which, considering all things, seems to have been confiding in him.[1] They were in Benin City for thirty days, but during this time their men, from drinking palm-wine

[1] Richard Eden gives rather a quaint description of this pepper, which is now called chili or red pepper. He calls it "the grain or spice of the country, which is a very hot fruit, and much like figs."

and other causes, were dying at the rate of four and five a day. This made Captain Windham send to tell them to return at once; but as they wished to wait longer till they had collected all their pepper, Windham sent them a second message to say that if they did not return at once he would sail away and leave them. Whereupon Pinteado returned with the intention of trying to persuade Captain Windham to stop.

Windham, however, before this, in his rage against Pinteado, had broken open the latter's cabin and spoiled all the "cordials and sweetmeats he had provided for his health," and taken away all his clothes. "After which strange procedure," Eden says, "he [Windham] fell sick and died." Pinteado also, after mourning for Windham as if he had been his dearest friend, and after having been still worse treated by the rest of the mariners and officers, fell sick and died likewise. Then this unfortunate expedition had to sink one of their ships for want of hands to navigate her, and eventually returned to England with scarcely forty out of the original 140 able-bodied men who had started in it. Poor Captain Pinteado must have been unlucky most of his life, for before leaving Portugal he seems to have suffered long imprisonment on a false charge. Amongst his papers was a quaint one, a Royal Patent appointing him one of the Knights of the Royal Household of Portugal, with a salary of ten shillings a month, and half a bushel of barley every day so long as he should keep a horse; but with an injunction not to marry for six years, lest he might have children to succeed in this allowance.

After this, though there were several English expeditions to the Coast of Guinea, none seemed to have reached Benin until 1589, or over thirty years afterwards. In 1588, the charter I have spoken of was granted by Queen Elizabeth to certain merchants of Devon, to trade between the Rivers Senegal and Gambia, or, as they were called then, Senega and Gambra. At the end of 1588 two worthy merchants of London, Bird and Newton by name, fitted out another expedition to Benin, consisting of one ship of one hundred tons and a pinnace, under the chief command of a Captain James Welsh, who made two voyages in succession to these parts and wrote the account of them. This expedition of one 100-ton ship and one pinnace seems rather small in these days, especially after the late Punitive Expedition, which consisted of two first-class cruisers of 12,000 tons, one second-class, three third-class, and three gunboats. Captain Welsh's expedition eventually left Plymouth on the 14th December 1588, and reached the mouth of the Benin River on the 14th February 1589. Here Anthony Ingram, the chief factor, and several of the others got into the pinnace and ship's boats and proceeded to Benin City. Gwatto, or, as they called it, Goto, seems to have been then, as now, the landing-place for Benin City, and there accordingly the party landed. They also seem to have been well treated by the reigning monarch, who promised them all the pepper, etc., they wanted. This was not the same king that received Captain Pinteado, for the present one stated

HISTORY OF BENIN

that during his reign no Christians had traded for pepper in his country, consequently that there wasn't much ready, but that he would have plenty of it ready for them when they returned next year. This expedition also suffered badly from fever, losing many men, including the son of one of the owners of the ship, and the captain, Hempsteed. They got back again to Plymouth in September the same year.

Captain Welsh started off again in September the next year, 1590, with the same ship and under the same owners. This time they reached the mouth of the Benin River about the 15th January 1591, and the captain and merchants went up the river as before in the small boats. They got all their cargo on board and sailed away for England by the 28th April, reaching England only on the 13th December. Each time the cargo they brought back was much the same,—elephants' teeth, bags of pepper, and barrels of palm-oil; while the "commodities" they took out are not so very dissimilar to those used in trade nowadays, namely, "broad cloth, kersies, bays [whatever they may be], linen cloth, unwrought iron, copper bracelets [called manillas, and used now by certain tribes in the Protectorate], coral [which is still much worn, and tremendously sought after by the chiefs and rich men of the Benin River], hawks' bells, horses' tails, hats, and the like."

In none of the accounts of these voyages is there any description of Benin City itself, but from a Dutch account written a few years later it appears to have been quite a magnificent city. The narrator talks of entering the city on horseback through a gate where there was a very thick high earthen bulwark, with a deep broad ditch, which, however, was dry and full of high trees. Later writers also speak of Benin City being surrounded by a high wall, but that seems to have disappeared long ago. The Dutch explorer quoted above, whose name, I believe, was Dantsic, also speaks of an enormous broad street running through the city, and other great streets running off it—so long that it was impossible

HISTORY OF BENIN

to see to the end of them. He also gives a description of the King's Court, which seems to have been very grand, of the number of horses the King possessed (nowadays no Benin City man has ever seen a horse, or scarcely heard of one, as there are none anywhere near it). The King also had many soldiers, many gentlemen, many slaves, and many wives—only about six hundred! Twice a year the King of those days went out of his Court and visited the town, accompanied by his six hundred wives. The gentlemen of Benin also had many wives—some eighty, some ninety, some more. These gentlemen seem to have been the aristocracy of Benin, and used to come to the Court riding on a horse, with a man on each side, to hold them on I suppose, and other slaves carrying big shields, to keep the sun off the gentlemen's heads, whilst yet more slaves made music for them, playing on drums, "hornes and flints,—some have a hollow iron whereon they strike." As all this music came immediately after the gentleman on his horse, it is no wonder that he had to be held on his horse, or, as the narrative puts it, "having on each side a man, on whom they hold fast."

Even in those days, though sacrifices are not mentioned, the chief executioner seems to have been a most important personage.

After this, Benin City was visited frequently by explorers and traders of all nationalities. And though at first the Portuguese seem to have been the paramount European Power, their language and names being used for a long time by the Benin people, they seem to have gradually disappeared from Benin City in the same way as they left all their places on the Gold Coast and other parts of the Central West African coast-line. The Dutch seem to have succeeded them; and a most interesting account of a visit to Benin City about the year 1700 by a Dutchman called David Van Nyendaeel is given by one William Bossman, a most worthy person, chief factor of the Dutch possessions in West Africa at that time, and the leading authority on that part of the world. Van Nyendaeel speaks in admiration of Benin City and its great long and broad

HISTORY OF BENIN

streets, and also makes mention of human sacrifices. In his days the Benin men were great makers of ornamental brass-work, which they seem to have learned from the Portuguese. Amongst other notable travellers of later days who visited Benin City were Belzoni, the great Egyptian traveller, who died at Gwatto in 1823, and also Sir Richard Burton, who seems to have gone to every place in that part of the world that was worth seeing and at all hard to get at.[1] Captain H. L. Gallwey, D.S.O., of the East Lancashire Regiment, who had been appointed Vice-Consul of the Benin River District, visited the city in 1892, and from his

[1] Sir Richard Burton, it appears, went up to Benin City with a missionary to try and put a stop to human sacrifices during the time that he was Consul at Fernando Po. In his time there was one horse in Benin City on which the King rode, being held on much after the manner of his ancestors. One chief was very disappointed at not getting a present of a carriage and pair of horses, which he was expecting daily as a present from the Queen of England. The missionary who was with Burton had taken up a small harmonium, and, by way of entertaining the King, Sir Richard Burton danced an Arabian dance before him, whilst the reverend gentleman played "We shall meet to part no more," on the harmonium. This, Burton says, was hardly appropriate, as his version would be, "We shall part to meet no more."

account Benin City was only the ruins of its former greatness; no fine broad roads, nothing but collections of houses here and there.

Of course, in the slave-trading era, Benin City, like all the big towns in the Protectorate, was a great centre for obtaining slaves, and I believe that Captain Gallwey's party saw the remains of an old slave barracoon close outside the city. With the abolition of the slave trade one great source of wealth disappeared, and by the stupidity of the King in stopping all his people from trading every now and then, most of the others disappeared also, till the once great Benin City became what the Punitive Expedition found it, namely, a very large collection of scattered huts scarcely superior to any ordinary village of those parts. The country in itself is rich enough in trade produce, such as palm-oil, kernels, etc., and about ten years ago there were several factories on the Benin River doing an excellent trade with the Benin City Country, but in the last few years the amount of trade has dwindled down to almost nil, and now the different firms have built fresh

HISTORY OF BENIN

factories at Sapele, some fifty miles up the Benin River, at the junction of the Jamieson and Ethiope Rivers, where three-quarters of the trade of the Benin River District now goes to.

Another source of wealth to the King of Benin used to be the Benin Juju. Juju in this case meant a very powerful spirit or god that lived in Benin City, and was represented by the King. So powerful was it that until about three or four years ago some of the big chiefs close behind Lagos, who, one would have thought, were civilised enough to know better, used to send an annual subsidy or tribute on account of the Juju. The Benin River chiefs did the same, but their tribute was partly to induce the King to keep the trade open.

Then, again, the King was supposed to be very rich in ivory, as he received, or was supposed to receive, one tusk of every elephant shot in his dominions; but this ivory he seems to have stacked in his houses instead of selling. His slaves also, owing to the amount of wretched human sacrifices perpetrated every year, must have been an expensive item in his accounts.

Both slaves and ivory came from the Sobo and Abracca countries to the east of the Benin City Country proper, but which were part of the Benin Kingdom. It is to be hoped when the country has got settled down after the late expedition that the trade will revive again, for the country, as I have said, is rich in all kinds of produce, palm-oil, kernels, rubber, kola nut etc. etc., and I fancy the people will be only too willing to open up trade when they find they can do it for themselves, and without let or hindrance from the King of Benin and his Juju men. Of course this will take some time, for, being so absolutely steeped in superstition, and having had so little intercourse with white men, it will be hard to make the people realise that their all-powerful Juju is a thing of the past, and no longer has any power over them. By their old Juju they were forbidden to leave their country or to cross water, consequently no Benin men could ever get into canoes, and in the days of trade had to rely on the Jakris and Ejaws, the two great trading tribes of this district. These two tribes act as middlemen between the English merchants and the tribes dwelling farther inland, and from whose country the palm-oil and other trade-stuffs come, and are very anxious to prevent the two—the white man and the oil-producer—from meeting. However, as year by year the country is getting gradually opened up, the part of middleman will be done away with to a great extent, especially in the case of the Benin City Country.

Of the farther parts of the Benin Kingdom in the Sobo plains and Abracca country not much is known, as, by the King of Benin's orders, no white man has been allowed to go any distance away from the Ethiope River, on the right bank of which it lies. A great deal has been done in the last few years towards exploring and opening up the country on the left bank of the Ethiope, and beyond that again by the Protectorate officials, notably Captain Gallwey, Major Crawford, and Mr. Locke; and now the opening up of the country on the right bank is only a matter of time. I believe that it was somewhere in the direction of this country that the King of

Benin and his counsellors fled after the taking of Benin City by the Punitive Expedition. By this capture was ended the ancient kingdom of Benin; and it is curious to think that a people who seem to have been more or less civilised in the sixteenth century, with a city that excited the admiration of all the Europeans of that date, should at the end of this nineteenth century have relapsed into a state of absolute savagedom, inferior to most of the peoples round them, whilst the wonderful city became a collection of half-ruined mud houses, not much better than the huts in an ordinary native village.

The same has been the case with other West African kingdoms which have been once famous, such as Dahomey and Ashanti, the rulers of which, having been more or less spoiled by the deference and attention shown them by the various white men who have visited their countries, have gradually become "too big for their boots"; and, imagining they were more powerful than any European nation, have by degrees and their conceited behaviour stopped the white men visiting them, and by so

HISTORY OF BENIN 17

doing have become almost as pure savages as they were before their first contact with Europeans. Wherefrom anyone can deduce a moral to suit whatever his private opinion may be.

I was in Coomassie, the capital of Ashanti, for a short time in April 1892, in command of the escort of a small expedition under Captain J. I. Lang, R.E., who was British Commissioner for settling the western boundary of the Gold Coast with the French. We had expected to find a respectable town, but saw nothing but a collection of small villages, the huts of which were nearly all in a half-ruinous condition. The huts that had been told off to us looked like sieves, and were altogether in a very tumble-down state. The King's palace was a good deal better, and he was building himself a palaver-house that was supposed to be something very grand, but after all it was nothing more than an extra large mud hut with the walls more carefully smoothed than usual. This king was of course King Prempeh, who was taken prisoner by our expedition in 1896. The only glory of

Coomassie was in the remains of the stone wall of the old palace, which was knocked down by our troops under Lord Wolseley in the war of 1875. Each of these stones had been brought from a distance of one hundred miles on the heads of natives, as there is no stone in the country, which made it of course extra valuable.

We certainly had a grand reception from some 12,000 to 14,000 men, and the King alone was a sight to see, being a mass of gold from a kind of fireman's helmet he had on to the tips of his sandals, which alone must have been worth some hundreds of pounds. Still, with all this reception there were no signs of any civilisation, and the Coomassies had relapsed into most of the usual customs of savages, which had at one time been stopped—particularly of human sacrifices, which led to the last expedition of 1896.

A peculiar thing happened during the latter part of this ceremony. The King, who at that time was a boy under twenty, I should think, and fat enough to have posed as a fat woman in a fair, condescended to dance before us, to the extreme and almost delirious

HISTORY OF BENIN 19

joy of his people, who get such a treat but rarely. In this dance he went through various actions with a toy bow and arrow, a toy gun, and other things, which actions represented that he was the best shot in the world with a bow and arrow, a gun, the strongest man in the world, and so on. Suddenly a Mr. Vroon, now a C.M.G., and one of the District Commissioners of the Gold Coast, who was with us, and who knew more about the manners and customs of the Ashantis than most people, held up two fingers, upon which the King more or less collapsed. Mr. Vroon explained to us afterwards that the King had been doing something which meant that the Ashantis were the most powerful nation in the world; the two fingers held up meant that England was more powerful, as shown in the '75 war, up to which date the Ashantis really believed that they could "lick creation." This '75 war had never been forgotten by either the Ashantis or by the many tribes released from their objectionable rule as the effects of that war; so, naturally, the King collapsed.

However, I am afraid I have wandered some way from the kingdom of Benin. Let its ashes rest in peace, so that there may be no more peaceful expeditions to it like our fatal one.

CHAPTER II

THE ROYAL NIGER COMPANY AND H.B.M.'S NIGER COAST PROTECTORATE

THERE seems to be a good deal of confusion at home between the Royal Niger Company and the Niger Coast Protectorate, so some explanation may be acceptable. The Royal Niger Company, a chartered company, started about 1885 by buying out—or amalgamating in itself—all the different companies, English and foreign, then trading on the Lower Niger. In the next year, 1886, they obtained their charter, and also the right to administer the country from the Nun mouth of the Niger as far as a place called Say, which was supposed to be the boundary between the Company's and French spheres of influence. Since then they have gone ahead rapidly, somewhat on the lines of the old East India Company, making treaties with all the big chiefs within their sphere, and by so doing stopping the advance of the French on the one side and the Germans on the other. Within their territory lie the great Haûsa States, Sokoto, Gando, etc. These Haûsa States are the result of a great Mohammedan invasion from the north some very long time ago, and the inhabitants are a very civilised race. They are all Mohammedans, and some of them can still write and read Arabic. The Haûsas are supposed to be the best-fighting race in this part of the world, and the Niger Company's constabulary are recruited nearly entirely from them. The principal stations of the Company, all of them on the Niger itself, are Lokoja, at the junction of the Benué with the Niger, and the headquarters of the troops ; Asaba, the administrative headquarters ; and Akassa, at the mouth of the Great River, and which was the scene of the attack on the Niger Company by the natives from Brass in January 1895. The coast-line of the Company lies between the Forcados and Brass Rivers.

The Niger Coast Protectorate, formerly called the Oil Rivers Protectorate, lies between our own colony of Lagos on one side, and the German colony of the Cameroons on the other, with the exception of the bit I have mentioned as belonging to the Royal Niger Company. The Protectorate is one mass of rivers large and small, and creeks by the thousand break the coast-line. The principal big ones are the Benin River, the Forcados, Brass,—one of the many offshoots of the Niger,—New Calabar, and Bonny, which are virtually offshoots of the Niger also, as they come from the Oguta lake, which is connected with the Niger, Opobo, Qua, Ibo, Cross, and Old Calabar Rivers. Between these are many small rivers useless for navigation, the mouths being too shallow to allow ships of any size to cross, and in addition for some thirty to forty miles inland the country is simply one network of creeks which join river to river. These creeks are more or less navigable for small steam-launches, so that it is very nearly possible to get from one end of the Protectorate to the other by water, land communication near the sea being practically nil.

The Protectorate of the Niger Coast was formally assumed in 1884, and was originally called the Oil Rivers Protectorate, from the fact of these rivers supplying the main part of the palm-oil exported from West Africa. At first it was administered by one consul, whose headquarters were at Old Calabar, and who had to do everything himself. In 1891 a proper Government was formed under an Imperial Commissioner, the first being Major (now Sir Claude) MacDonald, K.C.M.G., H.M.'s Minister at Peking. A vice-consul was placed in charge of all the important districts—Benin, Brass, Bonny, Opobo, and Old Calabar—with consular agents at those and other stations. A small force of soldiers was raised in 1891, 350 strong, afterwards raised to 450, whose headquarters are at Old Calabar, also the headquarters of the Government, with detachments at Sapele, Brass, and Degamah. The men are mostly Yorubas, with a fair-

THE ROYAL NIGER COMPANY

sized minority of Haûsas. Yorubas are supposed generally to be individually inferior to the Haûsas in the way of pluck, but, personally, I don't think there is much difference; and as a body of men I prefer the Yorubas, as they are steadier and more easily kept in hand, and consequently men better suited to the close bush-fighting of the country than the merry Haûsa, who is apt to get a bit out of hand at close quarters and delights in charging in with his knife individually.

From the large amount of country it is supposed to protect, and the number of different tribes to be dealt with, this small force sees a good deal of active service each year. Apart from numerous small expeditions, in one of which Captain Price, the late Commandant of the Force, was killed, it has taken part in conjunction with a Naval Brigade in three larger ones. The first against Nanna, the head chief of the Benin River, in 1894, in which it lost another officer, Captain Lawlor, R.M.L.I.; the second against the Brass natives, who had attacked and looted the Royal Niger Company's station at Akassa; and lastly in the late Punitive Expedition to Benin City, in which, being in front the whole time, they had most of the fighting, and in which, I am glad to say, Admiral Sir Harry Rawson, K.C.B., Colonel Bruce Hamilton, who commanded them, and everyone who saw them, spoke most highly of them. It is a most compact little force, too, possessing four 7-pounder field guns and three Maxims, one or other of which accompany every expedition. The 7-pounders are most excellent guns, as they are made to stand any amount of knocking about, and also to be mounted and dismounted in a very short space of time. They are much disliked by the natives of the country, who call them "them gun that shoot twice," referring to the explosion of the shells, which they consider distinctly unfair, taking place as it does so far away from the gun, and mostly unpleasantly close to themselves, when they are, as they fondly imagine, out of range.[1] Another thing they object to

---

[1] The native has also his pet name for the Maxim: "Them guns that goes pop, pop, pop, pop," etc. I once sat a friendly chief down behind one to show him how simply the thing

strongly is the war rocket, which they look on as an invention of the devil, and cannot understand how the wretched thing keeps on working its way through the thickest of forest, looking for them everywhere, as it were.

It is a peculiar country to deal with, the Protectorate, so far as its inhabitants are concerned, there being so many and various tribes with all their different languages and dialects. Thus a Jakri from the Benin River would be almost as much a stranger amongst the Old Calabar people as a white man. Then again, since King Jaja of Opobo was deported many years ago, and now that His Majesty of Benin has had to fly, there are no big chiefs by dealing with whom one could settle big tracts of country. It is a case of dealing with chief by chief, village by village, and it has often happened to officials trying to get through the country, exploring and opening it up, that though one village of a tribe might be most friendly and do everything in their

worked, and the old gentleman was so pleased that he wasted nearly five hundred rounds of our best ammunition before I could induce him to stop pressing the button.

power to help the white man, their own brethren of the next village would be the very reverse, and make him turn back again.

In the olden days of slave-trading, the Rivers, as the present Protectorate used to be called, was one of the great centres of that trade, and the big chiefs of Bonny, Opobo, and Old Calabar, the easiest places to get at, amassed much wealth in consequence. At such places, which are the headquarters of the district, and where they have been in touch with white men for some time, the natives are fairly civilised, especially now when many of the *jeunesse dôrée* come to England to complete their education, but the people living in between the rivers and farther inland are still savages pure and simple. As in the Benin River, so with all the other rivers, the natives living near the sea and near the various factories are the middlemen traders between the English merchants and the tribes living farther inland, who are the oil-producers. As it would mean the loss of their commission, the middlemen are very keen to prevent the white men trading with the actual oil-producers, and have been successful in doing so for many years by spreading such evil reports about the white man and what he will do, that the inland tribes are very shy about letting the white man come into their country. However, this is gradually coming to an end, as the country gets more opened up each year.

Although the languages are different, the manners and customs of the different tribes in the Protectorate are much the same. The great Mohammedan invasion, which came down from the north and founded the Haûsa States, stopped short at the River Benué, the big confluent of the Niger, and never reached the country now under the Protectorate, so that it is still the land of Juju. Juju here is everything, religion, superstition, custom, anything. And with it go such gentle customs as human sacrifices, cannibalism, twin-killing, and others. Of course all these customs are being abolished as fast as possible, and every year sees law and order brought into fresh big tracts of country where before all these brutalities used to take place. As far as human sacrifices are concerned, life in these parts, anyway the life of a slave, is not valued at much, and the gentle savage cannot understand why we should object to a few men being killed for a big man's funeral, or for some similar purpose, when such has been the custom of the country ever since there were people in it. Then the big man who is about to die also objects strongly, for he says that no one in the other world will believe that he has been a big man in this, unless he brings a certain amount of slaves with him to show what he can do in that line. He also thinks it is very hard lines that, after having spent so much money in celebrating his relative's funeral and in purchasing slaves for his own, he cannot do what he likes with his own goods and chattels. It is the anniversary of the death of the chief's grandmother's aunt, up go a few slaves; a new market is to be opened, up goes a wretched slave; nothing seemed to be celebrated properly in this Juju land unless it was accompanied by the death of some unfortunates. Of course I am talking about Benin City and such-like places, where the rule of the Protectorate had not yet reached, for if we could get at them there was always punishment for any town or village committing human sacrifices after having been warned not to.

Cannibalism was also one of the sweet things of the past all over the Protectorate. Even the Brass natives, who were a fairly civilised people, most of whom could talk English, and in whose town, Nimbe, there was a mission-station, with a sweet little church, were not beyond it. And after their successful raid on Akassa, mentioned above, most of them killed and ate the Kroo boy prisoners they had taken there. There was one brilliant exception, Chief Warri, now the head chief of that part of the world, who kept his prisoners, treated them exceedingly well, and sent them all down to the Vice-Consulate afterwards. Amongst the cannibals was the son of a chief just returned from England, where he had been for some years being educated in a missionary college. There happened to be a French father from the Roman Catholic Mission at Onicha on the Niger, in Nimbe, the capital of the Brassmen, at the time, who of course wasn't allowed to go away, but was otherwise well treated. This educated, civilised chief's son, waltzing about the town with a Kroo boy's leg over his shoulder, came across the father, and said, "Father, have a bit." Civilisation had not gone very deep.

The killing of twins is another wretched, insane custom that seems to have been in force for centuries, but which is also being stopped all over the Protectorate. The usual thing was when a wretched woman gave birth to twins for the babies to be killed or thrown into the bush to die, and the unfortunate mother to be driven away, never allowed to come near any town or village, and most probably to die of starvation in the bush. The house in which the twins were born, and everything in it, was destroyed, and the father had to pay sacrifices of sheep and fowls by way of purifying the village again. After that he could take another wife, but could never have his former wife back, or even see her again. Now villages, called twin villages, have been made in several places, where the unfortunate mothers can go and live, while the babies are saved and brought up by someone else.

By far the best work in this line has been done by a Miss Slessor, one of the lady missionaries from the Scotch Mission at Old Calabar. She has settled herself in a district called Okoyon, some way inland from the Old Calabar River, of which district she is virtually queen, as in it her word is law, and the natives, who adore her, do nothing without consulting her. She has taught herself to speak the language of the country as well as any native, and knows far more about the history and relationship of all the different chiefs of that part of the world than any one of the natives themselves. She has got such a hold over the people that all killing of twins and such-like evil customs have been absolutely stopped. When twins are born, Ma, as Miss Slessor is called by her people, is at once sent for. By washing the house and all its contents herself she is considered to have re-purified it, and is allowed to save the woman and take the twins back to her own house,—a house, by the way, that she has more or less built with her own hands. All this she has done entirely by herself in a very large district where, not many years ago, there was nothing but disorder and trouble. However, these things are nearly all things of the past so far as the Government of the Protectorate has been able to reach, and the natives are beginning to understand that it is better to live under law and order than in the old days when might was right.

Besides the various Consular Courts at the different Vice-Consulates, native Courts have been established over all the lower part of the Protectorate, presided over by the chiefs themselves. In fact, life altogether in the Protectorate has changed entirely in the last six years. In olden days the traders, who were, with the missionaries, the sole white inhabitants of the Rivers, used to live in hulks moored near the banks of the river. Now both traders and officials live in comfortable wooden houses, and, instead of the hard drinking carousals that one hears of in the past, every river has its cricket and tennis club.

One thing that has not changed is the climate. The Rivers was supposed to be the most unhealthy place in West Africa, which is saying a good deal. According to the old saying—

> The Bights of Benin, the Bights of Benin,
> Where few come out though many go in.

But I believe that by late statistics the average death-rate of the Protectorate is not nearly so high as those of our own colonies of the Gold Coast and Lagos. Of course the malarial fever of the country is bad, very bad, and seems to attack all sorts and conditions of men, temperate or intemperate, active or otherwise, which is not surprising to anyone who has been in a mangrove country, for at low tide the swamps of black mud that are left seem to pour out malaria. No one seems to have discovered yet what the mangrove is good for beyond making a dismal swamp and breeding malaria. The wood is so hard that it blunts the sharpest axe, neither will it float. It certainly is the home of the mangrove oyster, for at low water one can gather any number of oysters off the mangrove roots; but then no one will eat them, as there is a general idea that the mangrove oyster is teeming with malaria.

Up country it is very different, great forests with magnificent trees, silk, cotton, mahogany, what is called false mahogany, canwood, and others, making a glorious sight, especially when one comes to the high land up the Cross River, where one can get magnificent views over miles and miles of the surrounding country. Inside the forest, or bush as it is called, it is not quite so pleasant, the bush being so thick that one can see nothing, but has to stick to the native paths. However, I have tried to describe the West African bush elsewhere, so will not say anything more about it here. It is owing to this dense bush that one can get no big game shooting. There are plenty of elephants in different parts of the Protectorate, but one only comes across them accidentally. There might be elephants within a quarter of a mile of one, but, thanks to the dense bush they might just as well be five hundred miles off in regard to discovering their presence. There are also hippopotami on some of the rivers, a place called Itu being

THE ROYAL NIGER COMPANY 37

always a sure find, as there is always a herd of hippo there ready to be shot at, who seem to say, "It amuses them and doesn't hurt us," as they are invariably in the same place; and though many shots have been fired at them, I have only known of one being shot in the last three years. Plenty of ammunition, too, can be wasted on crocodiles, which abound in every river. They are not very satisfactory shooting, however, as they have a mean way, when hit, of struggling into the water and disappearing. After being dead for two days, and if not eaten by their brethren, people say the bodies rise again and float on the surface, but whether this is true or not I know not. At Old Calabar these brutes have got so tame, as it were, that they have several times taken away a person bathing amongst a crowd of others in water scarcely knee-deep.

Talking of Old Calabar reminds one that in this, the headquarters or capital of the Protectorate, has been the greatest change. Six years ago, beyond the traders' houses on the bank of the river and the missionary settlement on what is now called Mission Hill, there were few signs of civilisation beyond a barn-like building, which was the Consul's residence. Now it is admired by all visitors, for what is called the Consulate Hill has been cleared of all bush, excellent wooden double-storeyed houses built for the officials, and properly drained roads made in all directions. In addition it boasts of a European hospital, to which all white men, officials or traders, are taken when seriously ill, and presided over by four English lady nurses, who by their presence and their great care have already saved many a white man's life who in days gone by would have left his bones in West Africa, although the hospital has been in existence barely three years. There are also the headquarter barracks of the Protectorate Force, making a most picturesque little square, and as clean as any British regiment could keep them, while behind them is a native village built by the soldiers themselves for the accommodation of the ladies and children of the regiment, called Soldier Town. Every recruit, when he has joined long enough to save sufficient money, starts a wife, who is the reverse of an expense to him, as in addition to cooking his "chop" (*Anglice*, food), the women, especially Yorubas, who are born traders, generally manage to make some money for their husbands by trading, but also often manage to get those same husbands into trouble, for "Cherchez la femme" is not seldom the solution of a row, and many black Mulvaneys have, like him, got into trouble by not keeping out of the married quarters. The barrack square is also the cricket ground, and, though the boundaries are a little close for big hitters, an excellent ground it makes. There is generally a cricket match every Saturday, when the band plays, tea is dispensed, and the ladies from the mission and hospital come and keep the rude man from forgetting his manners and politeness. In addition, the hard-working and weary official can generally get a game of lawn tennis or quoits every evening; while the magic game of golf has not failed to make its appearance here, and the ardent and hot followers of the game use just as many bad words and grumble just as much at their exceptional bad luck as their brethren of the club at home.

Another of the glories of Old Calabar is the brass band of the Force, which they own in addition to the usual drum and fife band. The instruments for this brass band arrived about the end of March 1894, but at the end of 1896 they were able to play selections from the *Gaiety Girl* and other comic operas, in addition to enough dance music for the programmes for two balls which took place in Calabar at the beginning of January 1897. Not half of the bandsmen could make themselves understood in English, but all of them now read music, and after not much more than a week's practice will be able to play the very latest selection received by the last mail. This excellence, for excellence it is, is owing to their having had a most enthusiastic band-president in Captain Searle, one of the officers of the Force, and an equally enthusiastic and hardworking bandmaster in Mr. Lipman, a West Indian, who for some years was in the band of one of the West India Regiments, and has been trained at Kneller Hall, the Military College of Music in London. So much for playtime at Old Calabar.

On the different rivers it is much the same as at Old Calabar, but as a rule most of the officials are going the rounds of their respective districts, and always trying to get farther into the interior each time. This is especially so in the dry season, when the ground is no longer one continued swamp and each little streamlet not swollen up by the rain. The rainy season generally commences about March or April with a succession of thunderstorms, called tornadoes in West Africa, and lasts till about the end of October or the beginning of November, finishing up with another succession of tornadoes. Between November and March is the dry season, when, with the exception of a few storms, no rain falls. The dry season is also the hot season of this part of the world, and as a rule the end of it is the most unhealthy part of the year for Europeans. The rainy season is a bit cooler, but there is no doubt about its being a rainy season, for as a rule the rain comes down in seas from the sky, and I should be called a speaker of untruths if I mentioned the number of inches that have fallen in some periods of twenty-four hours. Anyway, the total rainfall is supposed to be the heaviest in the world.

There yet remains a certain amount of country in the interior of the Protectorate and west of the Cross River to be opened up, and at present the natives are very suspicious of the white man, and will not allow any white man through their various districts. At the end of last year, 1896, two of the Protectorate officials, Major Leonard and Captain James, managed to reach a place called Bende, some sixty miles into the interior from the head of the Opobo River, which no white man had been able to get to before. But their success was to a certain degree due to their having with them several chiefs of the Opobo River tribes who trade with Bende, and also to their being supposed to be the possessors of "big Juju" (powerful magic) in the shape of soda-water,

THE ROYAL NIGER COMPANY 43

the natives being much impressed with the corks popping out of the bottles with no apparent effort. It sounds silly, of course, but trifles like these often lead to the success of an expedition. And often in similar ones, unless one has a fairly strong force with which to impress awe and respect, to be successful one has to go through, according to the manners and customs of the country, what we consider all sorts of childishness; for one man alone, even though he be a white man, and in consequence a curiosity, is but a small man unless he has a big expedition at his back. When this interior country has been opened up and settled, the Protectorate will be in touch with the Royal Niger Company's stations on the Benué River, the great branch of the Niger, and in not many years to come will be, it is hoped, one of Her Majesty's richest and most valuable colonies in West Africa.

CHAPTER III

POSITION OF BENIN

THE kingdom of Benin lies somewhere between the latitudes of 5° to 6° N. and the longitudes 5° to 6° E. In olden days it used to reach right down to the coast-line, but how far inland to the north and east it is almost impossible to tell. Lately none of the Benin City Country touched the Benin River, but was bounded on the west and south by the Gwatto and Ilogi Creeks. Consequently, anyone who has not been there is apt to get somewhat confused in hearing of the different Benins. First of all there is Benin City and the Benin Kingdom, then the Benin River, near the mouth of which is what is called New Benin, consisting of the different factories and the old

POSITION OF BENIN 45

Vice-Consulate House, now only used as a Custom and Post office, and finally what is known as the Benin District, under a Vice-Consul, which comprises all the country around and between Sapele and Warri.

To take the river first, which is only called the Benin River for about fifty miles, as above Sapele, which is about that distance from the sea, two smaller streams join, one of which flows from the north, being called the Jamieson, and the other from the east, the Ethiope. The Jamieson is navigable for steam launches for about thirty miles to a place called Sapobah; from there small canoes can get up only a little farther, as the river becomes but a small stream too narrow for any navigation, and overgrown with big forest trees. The Ethiope comes into Sapele from the east, and was the south-east boundary of the Benin Kingdom. On the left bank are another tribe called the Sobos, who are the great oil-producers of this part of the world, and who also used to produce the majority of slaves for the Benin City people. Sapele has now become the headquarters of the government and trade of the Benin River, the Consulate and several factories having been moved there. It is a lovely place to look at, as there is a magnificent background of huge forest trees to all the different clearings, while on the other bank is one dense mass of foliage, the forest reaching right down to the waterside. Here, too, the water begins to become beautifully clear, and is studded every here and there with masses of water-lilies and small green islands made of water plants just peeping above the surface of the water. However lovely to look at, it is not quite so pleasant to live in, being, like all this part of West Africa, more or less unhealthy.

From Sapele a good road has been made across to Warri, about twenty-five miles distant, where is the other Protectorate Government Vice-Consulate of this part of the world. From Warri the great Niger River can be reached by water through what is called the Warri branch of the Niger, one of its numberless offshoots, and, in the event of the Niger River and Niger Coast Protectorate ever

POSITION OF BENIN   47

coming under the same government, would be a place of great importance, as the big main line steamers can get up easily to Warri from the Forcados River, while at present they have a little difficulty sometimes in reaching the Royal Niger Company's depôts at Boruta, situated on the left bank of the Forcados River, and Akassa, at the mouth of the river Nun entrance of the Niger.

To return to Sapele: about eight miles below is Warrigi, where the main column of the Naval Brigade was concentrated before the advance on Benin City. Seven miles north from Warrigi is Ciri on the Ilogi Creek, where the Niger Coast Protectorate troops were, and close to Ilogbo, a town on the other bank, and which was first attacked on the advance. The Ilogi Creek here was the southern boundary of the Benin Kingdom, and running up first east and then northwards comes from close to Benin City, and was the creek from which the inhabitants got their water. From Ciri it runs in a south-westerly direction, and eventually joins the

Benin River about twenty-five miles lower down from Sapele.

As one goes down the Benin River all the forest land and high banks gradually disappear, and the melancholy mangrove takes the place of everything. Some twenty miles from the sea is the entrance to what is called the Forcados or Nanna's Creek, the latter after Nanna, who until 1894, when he was smashed up and his town of Brohoemi burnt by a combined force of Naval Brigade and Niger Coast Protectorate Force, under Admiral Sir Frederick Bedford, K.C.B., was the head Jakri chief of the Benin River. This Forcados Creek is the waterway for steamers coming from the Forcados River and the sea, the bar of the Benin River being too shallow to let anything but small steamers come across it. Opposite the entrance to the Forcados Creek, which is on the left bank of the Benin River, is the entrance to the Gwatto Creek.

Farther down the river, on the same side as the Gwatto Creek, *i.e.* the right bank of the river, are two big creeks called respectively Adabrassi and Lagos Creeks, and amongst many others one important small one leading to Brohoemi, the town of Nanna, the chief mentioned above, and, as he thought, the only way of arriving at his town, surrounded by swamps as it was,—in fact, it was actually built on a swamp. Consequently, this creek was defended by a battery of big guns mounted behind a hidden stockade, most artistically screened so as not to be seen from the creek. This battery fired on H.M.S. *Alecto's* steam pinnace, which was reconnoitring up the creek, and very nearly sank her, the pinnace only reaching the *Alecto* in a sinking condition, and with everyone on board her, some six or seven, with the exception of her commander, Captain J. Heugh, badly wounded. Amongst these was Major Crawford, who was killed in the last fatal expedition to Benin City. Unfortunately for Nanna, the force, when they eventually attacked Brohoemi, waded through the swamp, generally waist-deep in mud, and attacked from the side Nanna least expected, and on which he had got but few of his guns trained.

To return to the Benin River: on the left bank, nearly opposite the entrance to the Lagos Creek, is the Deli Creek, the route that steam launches take going to the Forcados River, but which is too narrow for steamers. Passing the Lagos Creek, and on the same bank, we come very soon to the factories and the old Vice-Consulate, which are about six miles from the mouth of the river, and which are called, as I have said, New Benin. The Government House is only a Customs and Post-office station, part of the house and most of the outbuildings having been removed to Sapele; while, of the many factories that there used to be here, only four remain used, the rest being represented by a few remains, as trade at the mouth of the river has year by year sunk to something very small.

On the opposite side of the river to New Benin, and some way from the river bank up a small creek, is the town of Baterri, where Chief Dore, the head chief of the river since Nanna's downfall, lives. It is built on one of the few patches of solid ground to be found hereabouts, for the whole country near the coast-line is simply a network of creeks and mangrove swamp, any villages that there are being hidden some distance away from the banks of the river, or creek, and the only entrance to which is usually some insignificant-looking little creek. It is melancholy work sometimes steering through these creeks from station to station in a launch, going hours together without seeing a sign of a human being, and nothing to look at but the depressing mangrove and swamp, and smelling nothing but the still more depressing effluvia of the mud.

For many years past the only way of reaching Benin City was by Gwatto, which is about forty-five miles up the Gwatto Creek from its entrance into the Benin River. There the Gwatto Creek is about three-quarters of a mile wide, and surrounded by mangrove, but gradually one leaves that behind as the creek narrows, and when one gets to the Benin Country at Gwatto, or at Gilli Gilli, which is two or three miles nearer, one reaches once more the high banks, good solid ground, and forest country. At Gwatto the creek is only about forty or fifty yards wide, and comes down from the northwards, narrowing and narrowing the farther one gets up, till it dwindles away from the source, wherever that may be.

The Gwatto Creek might be called the western boundary of the late Benin Kingdom. The boundaries on the north and east I do not know, except that somewhere to the north are a tribe called Mahins, who were supposed to be enemies of the Benins, but toward the northeast, in which direction the King must have fled, the country was open to him, being part of the possessions of the late Benin Kingdom. Away beyond is the great Yoruba land, and plenty of the Yorubas, who are great traders, and semi-Muhammedans, used to trade in the Benin Country, and I believe the Yoruba language is more or less understood in Benin City. When this part of the Protectorate has been opened up and settled, it will join the hinterland of the Lagos Colony on one side, and the possessions of the Royal Niger Company on the other.

CHAPTER IV

OUR EXPEDITION

AFTER 1892 no white man, with the exception of Mr. M'Taggart of the Niger Company, has been allowed to visit Benin City. After the expedition against Nanna in September 1894 there was some chance of another expedition being sent to Benin City in the dry season of 1895, which falls in about February or March, but owing to many causes this could not be done.

Nanna was the head chief of the Benin River natives, a Jakri, and an extremely powerful and rich man. His town, Brohoemi, made by his father Alluma, was a most wonderful sight, the ground on which the greater part of it was built having been reclaimed from the mangrove swamp by millions of canoe-loads of sand poured on it. The whole place was kept extremely clean, and the houses built in streets running at right angles to the main road, broad as Piccadilly, which connected Nanna's own part of the town with his father's, Alluma, which lay some half-mile distant.

Brohoemi was approached by a narrow winding creek from the Benin River, which was some three-quarters of a mile distant. It is not necessary here to describe how the place was captured and destroyed by a naval and military expedition under Admiral Sir Frederick Bedford, K.C.B., and Consul-General Moor, K.M.G. Nanna before this expedition was the greatest and most powerful of all the trading chiefs in the Benin River, and his canoes used to visit all the different markets of the Benin City Country itself, and also those of the farther parts of it which were situated between the Jamieson and Ethiope Rivers, and as a consequence his name and prestige were well known to the King of Benin. Still, strong though he was, Nanna always paid the King of Benin a yearly tribute,

OUR EXPEDITION

partly on account of the powerful Juju of Benin City, and partly for trade to be kept open ; and neither he nor his Jakris would have dared to attack the King of Benin, for whom, and for whose men, the Jakris, like the Ejaws, and other trading tribes in that part of the world, have always had a most wholesome dread.

After Nanna's fall, the Benin City people were in much fear that they would be attacked in their turn, and, I believe, began making preparations accordingly. After some time the King began "putting Juju on," and closing all his markets, that is, preventing his people from bringing palm-oil and other trade produce down to the waterside villages, where the Jakris and others used to collect it. In answer to remonstrances from the Consul - General, the King of Benin consented to open a few markets, but demanded extra tribute from the Jakri chiefs of the Benin River, from Chief Dore, now the head of the River Dudu, and others, before he would allow all the markets to be open as before. His latest demand at the end of 1896, soon after Mr. Phillips had arrived in the Protectorate, was for some twenty thousand sheets of corrugated iron roofing for his houses.

At a meeting of the chiefs of the Benin River in November 1896, Mr. Phillips advised them to refuse to comply with this exorbitant demand. In 1894 Mr. M'Taggart, an official of the Royal Niger Company, visited Benin City unintentionally, so I was told. He was accompanied by a detachment of some forty soldiers and carriers from the Niger, and, according to repute, was misled by his guides to Benin City. He was, I believe, kindly received by the King of Benin, but I know no more about his visit than that he came back by way of Sapobah on the Jamieson River. From there, Captain Gallwey, at that time Vice-Consul of the Benin River, brought him and his men down by launch to the Vice-Consulate at Benin, and from that place the Protectorate yacht *Ivy* took him to Forcados, where he was put on board one of the Royal Niger Company's steamers.

During 1895 and 1896 several attempts had been made by Major Copland Crawford, the

OUR EXPEDITION

Vice-Consul of the district; Mr. Locke, who acted for him during his leave; Captain Maling, who was in command of a detachment of troops at Sapele, and others, to get to Benin City. They made their attempts from Gwatto and Ilogbo, the two main routes from the Protectorate, but all were in vain, as each time they were stopped by Benin City soldiers. By "stopping" is meant that they could go no farther without the certainty of fighting, which, of course, they were not allowed to do by very strict orders from the Consul-General. On one of these expeditions Major Crawford and Captain Maling landed at Gwatto with a detachment of twenty soldiers and some Jakri carriers. The white men and the soldiers were allowed to come into the town, but any wretched Jakri who showed himself was chased by the Benin City men, and hunted back to the waterside again.

During these years every opportunity was taken by the Protectorate officials of getting every information from natives about the Benin Country roads, creeks, water supply, etc.; but as all this came, of course, from native sources only, nothing reliable was known about the country except from Captain Gallwey's report of his visit in 1892. When Mr. Phillips, who had been appointed Acting Consul-General some six months before, arrived in the Protectorate about the end of November 1896, he held the meeting with the Benin River chiefs already referred to, and at the same time sent a letter to the King of Benin saying that he would be returning to that part of the Protectorate about the beginning of the New Year, and would much like to pay him a visit, as he was the most powerful king in the Protectorate. The object of the expedition was to try and persuade the King to let white men come up to his city whenever they wanted to. All their horrible customs could not be put down at once, except by a strong-armed expedition; but could be stamped out gradually by officials continually going up. Trade would also be opened up.

The expedition was arranged to start shortly after the New Year; and, to give notice of it, messengers were sent to the King of Benin a short

OUR EXPEDITION 59

time before that date, to carry him a small present (or, in West African phraseology, a "dash"), and to tell him that the Acting Consul-General (Phillips) was coming to visit the King, and would bring eight or nine other white men with him. The answer received to this message, which arrived after we had actually started from Sapele for Gwatto, was to the effect that "the King was extremely pleased at receiving the present, which he did not expect; but, at the same time, could not see any white men just then, as he was celebrating the 'custom' [West African for festival] of his father's death." This meant that he was engaged in sacrificing some hundreds of unfortunate slaves. "But," the message went on, "in one or two months' time he would send down, and let the Consul-General know when he was ready to see him; at which time he hoped that he [the Consul-General] would come, accompanied by one Jakri chief and by no other white men."

However, more of this message later on. All arrangements for the expedition had been made by the officials at Sapele; and most excellent arrangements they were, especially on the part of poor Kenneth Campbell, who was in charge of the carriers, and had worked like a slave at setting everything in perfect order. In consequence of the number of white men going,—each of whom had three carriers; two to carry baggage, and one for camp bed, and the extra food wanted for their maintenance,—the necessity of having to carry water for everyone, rations for carriers themselves, and for the drum and fife band of the Niger Coast Protectorate Force, which Phillips intended taking with him to make some sort of show, the number of carriers mounted up to some two hundred and forty. One hundred and eighty of these were Jakris, supplied by the different chiefs in the Benin and Warri Districts, and about sixty Kroo boys, supplied, some from the Government Consulate at Sapele and Warri, and the rest kindly lent from the different factories at both places.

These Kroo boys are the labourers of nearly all West Africa, and leave their country in thousands yearly to go and work at different

OUR EXPEDITION

places, returning after twelve months with their year's wages in the shape of clothes, singlets, hats of many and wonderful shapes, and other such-like articles calculated to rouse the admiration of their fellow-countrymen, and so useful for trade, money being absolutely useless on the Kroo Coast. They are a wonderfully cheery, hard-working race these Kroo boys, and very fairly honest, and the white men in West Africa would find it hard to do without them. The other natives of that part of the world have a very small relish for hard work.

All these two hundred and forty men we found that Campbell, with the help of Lyon (another Assistant District Commissioner of Sapele), had numbered and told off, each to the charge of his particular head man and load; in fact, Campbell had made all his arrangements as nearly perfect as possible. If it had been only on poor Kenneth Campbell's account, the expedition deserved to have succeeded.

Phillips left Old Calabar in the Protectorate yacht *Ivy* on Sunday morning, 27th December, accompanied by Captains Searle and Ringer of the Niger Coast Protectorate Force, who were going on a military expedition in the Isokpo Country up the New Calabar River, myself, and Mr. Powis, one of Messrs. Miller Brothers' agents at Old Calabar, who had lived at Gwatto for some time, and had been to Benin City on two or three occasions a few years previously. We left the military expedition at Degamah on the 28th December, returning ourselves to Bonny the same day. There we saw Captain Gallwey, who was at that time Vice-Consul of the district. It has been stated by several newspapers that if Captain Gallwey, with his knowledge of the Benin City Country and people, had known about this expedition, he would have persuaded Phillips not to go. Of course Gallwey did not hear the message received by Phillips afterwards; but at the time we met him he, like all the rest of us, never dreamt of anything serious happening, and thought we should be entirely successful.

Personally, from what I had gathered in long talks with Captain Maling about the Benin City people, I thought all along we should be stopped, most probably at Gwatto. That is, I expected we should be met by a body of Benin soldiers, and told we could get no farther. I had said so about a month previous to this to Phillips, and had bet him the large sum of £1 that we would not reach Benin City. He, poor old fellow, was most sanguine about our success. Of course if we had been stopped, it would have meant that, when sanctioned by the Foreign Office, the next expedition to Benin City would be an armed one, and we should have gone up with as many of the Force as could be spared from the different posts we had to keep up, and been prepared to fight if received with opposition. The King of Benin, in the treaty he signed with Captain Gallwey, had agreed to place himself and his country under H.M. Protectorate, and it was becoming a perfect disgrace that in the Protectorate, particularly in a part so close to one of our vice-consular districts, so terrible a state of affairs as that in, what was not very improperly called, The City of Blood should continue.

As regards my opinion about being stopped,

I learnt afterwards that this was shared by both Crawford and Locke. However, I fancy they, like myself, were only too ready to try any chance of getting up, none of us ever dreaming of anything so treacherously cruel as the massacre that took place. So absolutely treacherous was it, that it horrified all the surrounding tribes, who said, "It be monkey palaver, it no be man palaver," meaning that they never thought that any men could have behaved so treacherously.

We called in at Brass on the 29th December to land some troops to relieve a detachment there, leaving again the next day. From Brass also we took on board Captain Maling, who had been on detachment for a short time there, and also Dr. D'Arcy Irvine, whose time for going home on leave had arrived, and who came round with us as far as Sapele. As Dr. Elliot was going up on the expedition, Dr. Irvine took over his duties at Sapele temporarily, and consequently was the doctor who tended Locke and myself when we arrived back from the expedition as wounded fugitives. Irvine waited on afterwards for the Punitive Expedition, a division of which he accompanied up the Jamieson River.

The *Ivy* arrived at New Benin on the 30th of December, and at Sapele on New Year's Day. As Phillips was very anxious that some member of each of the big trading firms should come with us, he invited Mr. Gordon of the African Association, and Mr. Swainson of Mr. Pinnock's firm, both of whom accepted the invitation gladly. Mr. Swainson had visited Benin City several times already, once with Captain Gallwey; and had we been successful in getting there, his knowledge and information would have been of immense value to us. However, luckily for himself, though he didn't think so at the time, he was suffering so badly from rheumatism that he was unable to accompany us.

All the Jakri carriers were sent off on the 1st in their canoes, with all our stores, etc., with orders to meet us at Gwatto the next day.[1]

[1] On the 2nd of January, that is. The expedition left Sapele about 7 a.m. on the 2nd January in the two Protectorate launches, *Primrose* and *Daisy*, each of which was towing a surf boat or lighter, in which were our carriers and the drums and fifes.

There were Phillips, the Acting Consul-General; Major Copland Crawford, Vice-Consul of the Benin and Warri District; Mr. Locke, District Commissioner of Warri, and who acted as Vice-Consul for Crawford when the latter was away on leave; Captain Maling, of the 16th Lancers, and of the Niger Coast Protectorate Force; Mr. Kenneth Campbell, a District Commissioner at Sapele; Dr. Elliot, the medical officer of Sapele and Benin District; Mr. Lyon, also Assistant District Commissioner at Sapele, who accompanied us as far as Gwatto; Messrs. Powis and Gordon, and myself; and, leaving out the last mentioned, I think it would be hard to find a better lot of men the wide world over. Every one of them was fit and ready to go anywhere, and do anything. All of them were men, in polo language, "hard to hustle off the ball." One thinks to oneself that the whole continent of Africa is hardly worth one of such men's lives. However, I suppose plenty of men quite as good have lost their lives for as little, and they died doing their duty; so what more can one say?

OUR EXPEDITION

To continue the story: we had also with us two Government interpreters; both were coloured men. One of them, Herbert Clarke, afterwards escaped, and the other was Towey, who had been with Nanna when Brohoemi was taken. He was then taken to Old Calabar, and educated by the Protectorate Government for interpreter's work. He turned out exceedingly well afterwards. Both of these men went up in a kind of bicycling costume—blue knickerbockers, stockings, and cloth tennis shoes. Poor Towey! His swagger clothes were the cause of his death; as we heard afterwards that he was captured by the Benin men, who said they would have let him go if he had been dressed like a native; but being like a white man, he must be killed. We had also a guide,—a Benin City man, called Basilli,—who had fled from Benin City some years before, and who, I believe, was a scoundrel, as he must have known something of what was going on.

About 10.30 a.m., as we were steaming down the Benin River, we met Chief Dore, the head chief of the Benin River, in a canoe, with the messengers that had been sent to the King of Benin a few days before. They brought back the message already mentioned, namely, that the King of Benin was extremely grateful for the unexpected present he had received; but, owing to the annual "customs" being in the process of celebration, he hoped the Consul-General would defer his visit for one or two months, until he (the King) sent to tell him that he was ready to receive him. The King hoped he would come then, accompanied only by one Jakri chief and no white men. The messenger added, that as they were leaving Benin City they heard orders given for parties of soldiers to be sent to all the waterside towns; but as this was usually done whenever any white men arrived in the Benin City Country, no one thought any more of it. However, it made both Crawford and myself suggest that it would be advisable to send back the drum and fife band, as, owing to their uniform, the Benin people might think we were bringing soldiers, and this might well lead to a collision straight away. Phillips agreed to this, and accordingly

OUR EXPEDITION

the band was sent back in Chief Dore's canoe, luckily for them, as their only arms consisted of bandsmen's swords, and they could not have done much in the way of resisting men armed with guns.

We took the messengers with us in the *Primrose*, and the chief one of them, a Jakri, —whose name I am sorry to say I have forgotten, a most intelligent man,—informed Phillips afterwards, that just as he was leaving the King's house, the King had spoken to him very privately, and had told him that if the white men really were coming up, he (the messenger) was to come back as quickly as possible and inform him. This we took to mean that the King understood that we really meant coming to Benin City this time, and wanted to make preparations for receiving us.

The guess turned out more or less true, but the preparations he made (namely, those for the ambush and massacre) were hardly those we thought of. This man I met afterwards, when we were escaping in a canoe on the 9th January, and he told me that after he had taken Phillips' last message to the King he had to run away, as the Benin men wanted to catch and kill him; he certainly looked nearly as much of a wreck as we did that day, and we were fairly miserable-looking objects.

Chief Dore before he left us told us the Benin men meant to stop our getting to Benin City, and tried to persuade Phillips not to go on; but, as I have said before, all the Jakris fear the Benin City men so much that we thought nothing of his advice or warning. Chief Dore told me afterwards that though he advised us not to go on at the time he never dreamt of such cruel treachery as the Benin men showed. He only meant that he thought we should be fired on if we insisted on going any farther than Gwatto. It was he that first used the words I have already quoted: "It be monkey palaver, it no be man palaver."

CHAPTER V

OUR EXPEDITION (*continued*)

ON leaving us Chief Dore went on to Sapele, taking the drums and fifes back with him, while we proceeded on in the two launches down the Benin River as far as the entrance to the Gwatto Creek, reaching there about midday. Another of the big chiefs of the Benin River District, Chief Dudu by name, lives about four miles up the Gwatto Creek, but, like all the towns of the district, his has to be approached by a small creek leading out of the Gwatto Creek. Phillips wanted to see Chief Dudu, but as it was very low tide when we arrived at the entrance of the narrow creek, at which time only the smallest canoes can get up, and as we hadn't any time to spare, a message was left for Chief Dudu to follow us up and come on to Gwatto.

Starting off again, we arrived at 4 p.m. at Gilli Gilli, the first Benin village on the Gwatto Creek, which is about one and a half mile from Gwatto itself, and about thirty-five miles from the Benin River. The Gwatto Creek, which at its entrance to the Benin River is some three-quarters of a mile or more wide, at Gilli Gilli narrows down to about fifty yards wide, but with plenty of water, eight to ten feet or more, for launches.

Immediately on our arrival at Gilli Gilli, the first thing done was to send the same messengers back to the King of Benin with the following reply from Phillips:—" The Acting Consul-General had received the King's message, and was very pleased to hear that his friend, the King of Benin, had been gratified with the present sent up to him. As he had accepted this present, it proved the King was the white man's friend, and he [the Acting Consul-General] was now coming to visit the King with nine other white men, and was bringing a much larger present with him. He regretted he could not wait two months, as the King suggested, but he had so much work to do in other parts of the Protectorate that he was obliged to come up now, as there were several matters he wished to talk over with the King."

As soon as a canoe had been obtained for them the messengers left at once, *i.e.* about five o'clock, and were to reach Benin City the next day. Another message was sent for a man called Dudu Jerri to come down and see the Acting Consul-General. This Dudu Jerri was the head man of a big village of Jakris settled at the waterside below the Benin town of Gwatto, and was a great friend of the Benin City people. In fact, he was supposed to be too much so at times, as he was suspected of giving them information of every expedition that left the Benin River with the object of trying to get to Benin City. This information he would get from his people when they were trading at the different factories on the river.

Dudu Jerri turned up soon after, and he was

also full of warnings and forebodings, all of which we laughed at at the time. He declared that Gwatto was full of Benin soldiers, who wouldn't let us land there, and would fire on us if we attempted to do so. However, he was sent back to Gwatto to tell the chief of the town and his people that "we were coming entirely on a peace palaver; that the King of Benin was our very good friend, having just accepted a present from us; that we were bringing him a still bigger 'dash,' and that we were only going to Benin City to see the King in an entirely friendly way." He was also bidden to tell them to have some quarters ready for us on the next day.

At Gilli Gilli we found all our Jakri carriers had arrived with their canoes and our stores, etc.; and soon after we arrived, three or four of us, including Phillips, Crawford, and myself, landed to look at the place. We found it was only a very small village of about ten half-ruined huts, deserted entirely except for an elderly female, who received us in the most friendly way. She informed us that all the men had gone away, as they were frightened. It was suggested at one time, by Crawford I think, that we should land our carriers and stores here, and let them march round to Gwatto, so as to avoid the trouble which would be caused by the ladder at Gwatto, which we had heard such a lot about from Crawford and Maling. However, the suggestion was not carried out.

By the way, while on the launch, we had all been busy learning from the messengers who had been up to Benin the proper form of salutation. This consisted of making three circles with the right hand closed, thumb pointing upwards over the palm of the left hand held open, then rubbing the two open palms together, and at the same time nodding slowly and gravely like a Chinese mandarin. Poor Crawford tried this salutation on the Benin men when they were shooting at us, but, alas, it was of no avail.

We had a very cheery dinner that night, all the ten of us dining together on the steam launch *Daisy*.

On the morning of the 3rd of January Dudu Jerri came back from Gwatto to say that the Gwatto Chief had got a house ready for us to sleep in, and was very glad to hear we were coming. We didn't leave Gilli Gilli till about midday ourselves, but our Jakri carriers were employed clearing the creek of weeds and cutting down branches which were likely to interfere with the launches, as about here the creek became very narrow. It was only about twenty minutes' steaming to Gwatto, but on arriving there Phillips decided not to land till about 4 p.m., when it would be cooler.

At Gwatto, as at all other Benin cities situated on the waterside, there are two villages of the same name, one being that of the Benin City men, built some little distance away from the creek on the top of the bank, which averages, I should think, from twenty to thirty feet high, and the other being a waterside village of the same name, which consists of a few huts occupied by the Jakris and Ejaws trading at that place. As I have said before, these trading tribes have a most wholesome dread of the Benin City men, and always make their big and more permanent villages on the other side of the creek, a few men only living on the Benin side to collect the oil, etc. that is brought down, and to take it over to their brethren on the other side, who paddle it down to the factories on the river. A few years ago there were two factories at Gwatto, the agent for one of which had been Mr. Powis, who was with us now; but in consequence of the King of Benin stopping trade, both of the factories had to be given up, and when we went into Gwatto itself we saw not a vestige of either of them, not even a signboard that Mr. Powis expected to see, announcing that it (the signboard) was Messrs. A. Miller Brothers' factory.

The carriers arrived very soon after the launches, and Campbell at once proceeded to get all the stores, etc. landed. Meanwhile some of our demon photographers—I believe there were six or seven cameras amongst our party of nine—began taking photos of everything they could get within range of. Amongst our photographers was a Mr. Baddoo, a man from Accra, on the Gold Coast, the Consul-General's chief clerk, and quite one of the nicest and most civil educated West Africans I have ever met. Poor chap! I don't know what his fate was, but he will be a great loss to the Protectorate. All the cameras fell into the King of Benin's hands with the rest of all our stores and baggage, and must have greatly exercised His Majesty's mind as to what they could be for. However, I suppose it was put down to "white man's Juju," like everything else the West African can't understand the use of.

Before we landed, Phillips issued a few orders, the first being that the Acting Consul-General would invariably march first, preceded by the guide and an interpreter. The other interpreter was to remain with Campbell, who, having his long line of carriers to look after, would be generally in the rear.

Another order was to the effect that officers might carry revolvers, but must not show them, for fear of frightening the natives.

As it is, to put it mildly, rather warm work walking in the middle of the day in that part of the world, one generally marches with one's coat off, and consequently one has no chance of hiding a revolver. This is why none of us had our revolvers out the next day. I have mentioned this detail here, as more people have asked questions about the matter than about anything else. Whether we could have fought our way back or not had we had them out, is a matter of opinion, and one that need not be argued out here.

We landed soon after 4 p.m., leaving Campbell and Lyon to bring up the carriers later on, and started for Gwatto proper not half a mile off. The path goes along the bed of a stream, at that time of the year nearly dry, with perpendicular walls of clay about fourteen to fifteen feet high on each side. After three hundred yards of this, one is stopped by the path ending in another perpendicular wall. To get on this is a ladder made very roughly out of branches of trees, by way of steps, fastened to two strong uprights.

The whole approach to Gwatto would make an excellent defensive position, as any force, before they got out of the path leading up to the ladder, would have little or no chance of returning any fire from men ambushed on the banks, and again would have a very hot time of it while climbing up the ladder. After which it would be ordinary bush-fighting.

However, this advantage was all counteracted when the Naval Brigade attacked the place during the late Punitive Expedition, by a judicious use of shells and rockets searching through the bush. Rockets especially are things the West African cannot stand.

On arriving at the top of the ladder we had, to some of us, our first meeting with Benin City men. These men were all Juju priests, and seemed extremely pleased to see us. They then proceeded to give us the "freedom of the country" (much freedom we got out of the country) by washing our boots. Phillips asked if they would prefer to wash our bare feet, and being told they would, we all, with the exception of Powis, who had received the "freedom of the country" some years before, proceeded to take off our boots and socks and have our feet washed. This interesting ceremony concluded, the Juju men asked for the customary "dash" (present), or perhaps "backsheesh" would describe it better, but were informed they could not get it until our boxes arrived.

After passing under another Juju in the shape of a newly-killed fowl, we arrived at Gwatto. In the old days, when white traders lived here, I believe it had been quite a flourishing place, but now it looked very deserted. It consisted merely of some forty or fifty dilapidated-looking huts made of red clay with bush growing up between them.

The Chief of Gwatto's house, where we slept that night, was very much superior, the walls, which were very thick, being polished till they were nearly as smooth and shiny as glass. Crawford and Maling, who had been here two or three times before, found several friends in the place, including a Benin City chief called Mary Boma, a young man about twenty-five.

He and another Benin City chief had to live at Gwatto permanently to see the chief of the place didn't do any trading on his own account, and they stopped trade whenever they were ordered to do so by the King. Mary Boma, if he is ever caught, should be hung, as he pretended to be a great friend of the white men, especially Crawford, whom he had told that he wanted to run away from his own country and come to live with him at Warri. Mary Boma must, of course, like all the rest, have known of all the preparations being made for us on the next day; but in spite of all his protestations of friendship he couldn't, or rather wouldn't, give his old friends one word of warning.

As soon as we arrived in Gwatto, we were taken to the Chief's house. The Chief himself was away at Benin City, to which place he had been sent for by the King. But he was represented by his son, rather a nice-looking youth about seventeen or eighteen, who received us extremely well, welcomed us most warmly, and informed us that we could have his house to sleep in that night, and that he and his people would do everything for ourselves and our carriers that lay in their power. By the way, during our stay in Gwatto we saw absolutely nothing of the soldiers that Dudu Jerri informed us were swarming in the town, and this made us believe that that gentleman had been lying on his own account to try and stop us from making friends with the Benin people, and also, coupled with several other circumstances, made us believe that they really did mean to be friendly.

After having talked some time with the young Chief of Gwatto, he informed us that the King of Benin had sent down three big men of Benin City to escort us there. These three gentlemen were then introduced to us, and, though very like monkeys in personal appearance, they looked quite a superior class of animal to the Gwatto people. They were all three rather elderly, grave, and most respectable-looking men. They informed Phillips that the King had sent them down to escort us up to Benin City, but hoped that we would wait at Gwatto for two days, so that they could send up and let the King know in time for him to make his preparations for receiving us. If we could only have known what preparations they meant, all those valuable lives might not have been thrown away.

Phillips in his answer said the same as in all his speeches, to the effect that the King of Benin was the good friend of our great white Queen, in consequence of the treaty he had made with her five years before; that he was also his (Phillips) good friend, having just accepted a present from him; and consequently that in visiting his friend, the King of Benin, he had brought no soldiers, but was bringing him a much bigger present, and that he felt sure that once the King had seen and talked with the white men, he would like to have them in his city and his country. He (Phillips) regretted much that he couldn't wait at Gwatto for two days as he had been asked to do, but he had so much work to do elsewhere that he couldn't afford to lose a day, and so must start early the next morning.

OUR EXPEDITION 85

After a little argument between the King's messengers and Phillips, the former trying to persuade him to stop another day, and the latter trying to make them understand that that was impossible, the messengers at last agreed to come with us the next morning, and to send off a messenger at once to Benin City to say we were starting the next day. As it was then about 5.30 or later, this messenger had to be provided with a lamp, a bottle of gin, a piece of cloth (these two latter being the usual "dash"), and one of our walking-sticks as a sign we were really coming. Phillips offered his ring at first, but the messenger wanted something bigger than that, and accepted the offer of my Malacca stick that I had had since 1885,—needless to relate, I have not seen that stick since.

After this we were all introduced by Phillips to the messengers with the titles of our various offices. Soon after this the palaver ended, and we parted from the King's messengers apparently on the most peaceful terms. The Chief of Gwatto was as good as his word; and when our carriers arrived, his people showed them where to get wood, water, etc., and did anything they could for them. We had another very cheery dinner that night, the last for all the poor fellows who were killed. Oh, if we could only have guessed or been told what was to happen the next day, and gone back then, and so saved all those good lives! But everything seemed so peaceful, and everything seemed to point out that the King had resigned himself to the necessity of allowing white men to come up to his city. None of us had the slightest suspicion of anything being wrong.

Personally I still had doubts as to whether the King's messengers would turn up the next morning to escort us; but when they did, and we were received in such a friendly way at all the different villages we passed, all doubts vanished, and I thought we were really going to get to Benin City. As for anyone giving us a hint, certainly Dudu Jerri had done so; but as the hundreds of soldiers he spoke about in Gwatto had apparently turned out such a myth, the rest of his warnings were taken to be of the same description.

The one man who might and ought to have guessed there was something wrong about the whole business, was Basilli, our guide, and who, as I have said before, was a Benin City man. He had run away from them some years ago to Sapele, where he had been taken on and given some sort of employment. When Gallwey visited Benin City in 1892, Basilli went with him, and from all accounts seems to have behaved none too well that trip. There was some reason for his not talking to his own people except when interpreting for Phillips, as they were apparently none too fond of him, seeing that he was a man who had left his country, consequently, according to their ideas, was more or less of a spy. Anyway, we never saw him talking to the Benin people; but it seems almost impossible to believe that, when the whole countryside knew about the ambuscade arranged for the next day (and they undoubtedly did know), Basilli could have failed to guess from signs and words that something was wrong. All he did was to take every opportunity of sitting at Phillips' feet, whispering yarns about Benin manners, customs, etc.

It was a picturesque scene that last dinner of ours,—ten of us seated at a table brought from one of the launches and placed on boxes, lit by some tiny lamps Campbell had brought up for the purpose, and placed just outside the entrance to the King's house. Behind us was a goodly pile of our stores lit up by native oil-lamps supplied by the Chief. These consisted of flat brass and clay dishes, containing palm-oil, in which a strip of cloth well saturated with oil lying anywhere in the dish performed the duties of wick. In front of us were ranged all our carriers, each gang rejoicing over a big wood fire. The multitude of these fires made the dark night as clear as day.

It happened then to be what is called in West Africa the Harmattan season, when a cold dry wind blows strongly at night. The Harmattan wind, cold as it is, is reported to blow down from the great Sahara, and brings clouds of dust, or rather sand, with it, and makes one feel very dry and cracked about the cheeks and lips in the early morning. Old coasters, *i.e.* white men who have been out on the West Coast for many years, will tell you that the effect of the dryness is such that when the Harmattan has been blowing particularly strongly they have seen cane chairs and sofas get up and dance about the room,—but old coasters, like other travellers, see various and wonderful sights at times.

In consequence of the Harmattan we all turned into bed fairly early in the Chief's house.

CHAPTER VI

OUR ESCAPE

WE were all ready to start at 7 a.m. on the 4th of January, and said good-bye to Lyon, who, luckily for himself, but much against his wish, had to return to Sapele. He went back in the launch *Daisy*, leaving the *Primrose* behind at Gwatto waterside, in case she was wanted to take any messages. The *Daisy* was to return in about a week, as we hoped to be back in about seven or eight days, which would have given us three or four days at Benin City.

It is worth while relating here that on the evening of this day, and after the massacre had taken place, some Benin men came down to the waterside, and, calling out to the engineer of the *Primrose*, told him that the white men who had gone up had sent them down to tell him to go back and bring back the other white man, as they wanted him. Though unaware that any disaster had happened, the engineer said his orders were to stop for the white men, and he could take no different orders from any-one else; and stop he did until some unfortunate carriers came down who had escaped, and told him that all the white men and nearly all the carriers had been killed. Even then I believe all he did was to get up steam and keep cruising about in case anyone came down, until he was ordered back to Sapele. It is curious that the Benin City men didn't fire on the launch, as it was anchored only about fifteen yards away from the landing-place, but they didn't.

Before we left Gwatto, Phillips had received many petitions from the Gwatto people for "dash" for all they had done for us. The Juju men who had washed our feet the day before were especially anxious for their fee. But in each case he answered that they would all get it when we came back. They looked rather blue at this, but daren't say anything. They knew what was in the wind, and expected that their share of booty from our stores would be a very small one, as nearly everything was going to Benin City.

Having then paraded our carriers, and being joined by the Benin City messengers, we left Gwatto about 7.30 a.m., amongst others who came with us being Crawford's friend Mary Boma, who was in the highest of spirits all day, and seemed to display tremendous friendship for Crawford and Maling. He came up, laughing and joking with them every time we halted. Unfortunately I lost the few notes I made during the morning, and cannot name the different villages we passed by. The road, or rather path, we went along was rather broader than the usual West African bush path, but only fit for marching in single file. It was the dry season, and, being still fairly cool during the day, it made walking much more pleasant.

Our order of march was as follows:—First came our guide Basilli, the Benin City man.

Then followed Jumbo, a civil policeman who was Phillips' orderly, in blue uniform. He carried the Consul-General's flag, a blue ensign with the Protectorate crest in the corner. After him came Herbert Clarke, the interpreter I have already spoken of. Then came Phillips, Crawford, myself, Maling, who was making a survey of the road, Locke, and Elliot. Powis and Gordon during the morning were some way back at the head of the line of carriers, with Kenneth Campbell, who kept walking up and down the long line of men to see they kept up. Hard work it was for him too, I expect, for with the gaps opening up between them they must have taken up nearly a mile of road.

Our escort of Benin City messengers soon disappeared in front, as we walked slowly, to prevent as much as possible straggling amongst the carriers. The road was an excellent one, smooth, level, free from creepers and roots, and quite unlike the ordinary run of bush paths in West Africa, which are generally overgrown top, bottom, and both sides, so that while you are trying to prevent a twig from putting your eye out, you run hard up against a sharp stick, or perhaps, while you are dodging something else, an unseen creeper or root in the path will catch your foot and send you head foremost into the bush. Let me mention here that "bush" is West African for dense forest, a broad belt of which runs down a large part of the West African Coast close to the sea. It is a hard thing to describe for one who has no gifts of description; but if one tries to imagine a thick wood in which big and little trees all intermingle their branches, with a tremendous dense undergrowth of shrubbery of all sorts, with brambles and various other evildoing thorns, all woven together into a maze so thick that neither man nor beast can press through it, one comes somewhere near the idea.

We passed three villages during that morning's march, halting at each, or rather at the place where the road to the villages joined ours, so as to let the carriers close up. All of these roads were fine clean paths, broad enough for two coaches abreast, and the villages were generally about four hundred yards away down them through the forest. All the streamlets, if there were any, being dry, the water supply of the villages consisted of reservoirs of rain water, made out of smooth hard-beaten clay. If we had had to depend on these villages for our water supply we should have drunk the whole countryside dry in a day; but we had brought enough water with us to last the whole of the expedition, ten days. It meant of course an extra number of carriers, but was quite necessary. At each village, as we halted, some of the men came out to welcome us, grinned all round their black faces, and seemed very pleased to see us,—knowing as they did what was in store for us, for I suppose they all expected to get a share of the forthcoming loot.

In nearly all the approaches to the villages we noticed a few kola trees growing. There is a tremendously large trade in kola-nuts over all West Central Africa, especially among the Haûsas and other Mohammedan tribes of the interior, who value it especially for its endurance-making qualities. However, it is not necessary to say any more about it, as the kola-nut and its virtues have already been described many times by men who have studied the subject scientifically, and know a lot about it.

During our march in the morning we had met several men going and returning along the road, but of course we thought nothing of it at the time. One whom we especially noticed was the Chief of the second village, as he had on an old red tunic with white metal buttons, with South Cork Militia, I think, on them. We noticed also that a couple of big patches close to the road had been cleared, *i.e.* cut down, why or wherefore we couldn't then guess; nor can I now, unless the Benin men proposed making their ambush there, and altered their plans afterwards. These places couldn't have been cleared for the purpose of making plantations, as the West African of that district never by any chance makes his plantation or farm so close by a road. It is always some way off, and approached by very narrow paths.

OUR ESCAPE

As it was about 11 a.m. when we reached the third village, we decided to halt and have breakfast, having marched only about seven and a half or seven and three-quarter miles by Maling's calculations. Here we were joined by the three Benin City messengers and also by Mary Boma, the latter of whom, I noticed on his arrival, was led away by the men of the village for a very secret mysterious talk. Though I told Phillips of it at the time, neither of us thought of anything suspicious about the incident, for everything had seemed so absolutely peaceful, and we had been so warmly welcomed everywhere along the road.

But again at this place, Basilli, our guide, must have heard something of the talk, for the meeting of these men was not very far from where we were sitting, and Basilli was as usual squatting at Phillips' feet, telling him about Benin "customs."

We had a great crowd to look at us here, including some of the ladies of the village. Any empty bottles, cigarettes, and pinches of tobacco seemed to be most welcome presents, and thankfully received. We did not move on again till 1 p.m., having had the last meal for so many of us,—worse luck,—and the last drink for Locke and myself for five weary days.

Our Benin City messengers, with Mary Boma and others who had escorted us from Gwatto, had already gone on, giving as an excuse for not waiting for us, that we walked quicker than they did, and would catch them up. We passed two more villages, at the second of which we halted for a couple of minutes to let the carriers close up, and soon after that we must have walked past nearly a mile of Benin City warriors in ambush. A very well-arranged ambush, from their point of view, it must have been too, for, though they were scarcely twenty yards from the road on our right-hand side as we advanced behind a bank, we never saw or suspected anything of their presence.

About here the bush was much thinner. I don't think it had been cleared lately, as I saw no signs of recent cutting, but some

OUR ESCAPE

time before, and the path was rather deeper, that is, the banks on each side of the path were a little higher. We had done, according to Maling, something over six miles since lunch, or about fourteen miles altogether from Gwatto, and were very nearly half-way to Benin City. Phillips intended halting for ten minutes to rest at the next village, and it was arranged that we were to sleep at the one beyond that. I am sorry to say that I have forgotten all the names of these villages, as I was relying on filling up my diary from Maling's sketch that night.

By this time, I fancy, we were all certain that we were going to get to Benin City, and just before the attack began we had been talking about celebrating poor old Crawford's birthday, which was to be on the 6th, two days hence, in Benin City; and we talked of how we would first drink Her Majesty's health, the first time it would have been drunk by such a large party of white men in Benin City, if not the first time altogether in that place; then Crawford's health, and so on.

It was then about 3 p.m., and we were walking in much the same order as when we started, except that Locke had stopped behind to tie up his bootlace, when suddenly a shot rang out a few yards behind us, to be followed immediately by a fusilade, that seemed to go back almost to the last village we had passed.

I have already explained how it was that we were not carrying revolvers, because we had orders not to show them; and as it was hot work walking in the middle of the day, we had our coats off, and were marching in shirt sleeves, which made it impossible to conceal a big weapon, consequently our revolvers were all locked up in our boxes. It is strange that the Benin men should have let the first lot of white men pass, and opened fire on the head of the carrier column; and what their idea was I do not know, for they showed no hesitation in firing at the white men afterwards.

At the first shot we couldn't believe that the firing was in earnest, and thought, as someone suggested, that it was only a salute in our honour. However, that idea was soon exploded by the cries from our wretched carriers, and yells from the Benin men. As soon as we were certain what it was, I sang out that I was going back to get my revolver, and Crawford said he would do the same, but poor old Phillips, for some reason of his own, said, "No revolvers, gentlemen."

Crawford accordingly stopped with him, but I insisted on going back. I called out for my boy Jim, who had been a very short distance behind carrying my coat and keys, but I am afraid he must have bolted at the first shot and got caught and killed by the Benin brutes, for I never saw or heard of him again, and his body wasn't one of those killed by the first volley, for I searched for him. Poor Jim! about one of the best servants I have ever had, black or white. He was a Kroo boy, a perfectly honest fellow, quiet, and always present when you wanted him (except this time, of course), and never in the way when you didn't want him. As I couldn't find Jim or my keys, I went farther down the path to try and find the box with my revolver in it, with the idea of breaking it open.

Turning a corner, I came on the effects of the first volley. On a strip of road about fifteen yards long were the bodies of some six or seven of our unfortunate carriers lying on the road. They must have been shot dead by the first discharge. Their heads had been cut off at once by the Benin men with machêtes, which are pronounced matchets (not hatchets, as the papers would have it.) These are long knives about two feet in length, and sent out from England as articles of trade.

Impossible as it sounds, one poor chap was sitting on the ground straight up, but with no head.

It was more or less impossible to find my box now, so I turned back to rejoin the others.

I hadn't gone far when I met them all coming back my way. Not seeing Phillips, I asked where he was, and was told by Crawford, and then by Jumbo, Phillips' orderly, that he had been shot dead. We decided to try and get back along the fourteen miles of road to Gwatto—a hopeless scheme, as one can see now, as these Benin warriors would have been able to keep in the bush parallel with us, shooting us down as we went along.

However, there was mighty little time for thinking what to do, and it seemed to us the best plan which offered. With us now were a whole lot of our servants, though my boy Jim unfortunately wasn't one. Baddoo, the chief clerk I have already mentioned, was there also, with another Baddoo, the Consul-General's cook, and Joe, Phillips' servant, all three of them being Gold Coast men. Herbert Clarke, the interpreter, and Jumbo, the orderly, also joined, and as we went back along the road several of our poor carriers who had bolted into the bush at the first volley kept picking us up. I saw one of them, quite a small lad too, hoist a "pal" of his on his back who had been wounded in the leg, and take him along—a plucky thing of the boy, for, besides being quite a youngster, he was a Jakri, and belonged to the tribe who funk the Benin men badly. Moreover, these same Benin men were shooting at him and all of us at the time.

There were three of the white men missing; poor old Phillips, who had been killed already, together with Mr. Gordon and Kenneth Campbell, neither of whom I had seen since breakfast-time, as Campbell was, as usual, looking after his carriers, and Gordon had, I think, been walking with him. I may mention here that there is no doubt that poor Kenneth Campbell was killed at once, and that all the various reports that were spread about his being captured and killed after two days, and some of which unfortunately got into the newspapers, were absolutely untrue, and nothing more than what we call "steamer yarns," which is West African for false reports and such-like.

As we went along, the Benin fiends kept up a running fire at us, and we kept on rushing up to them, trying to stop them by saying, "Adoo, adoo?" which is Beninese for "How do you do?" "Don't fire, you silly fools; it's all a mistake; it's a peace palaver," and other similar expressions; and it was about here that poor

Crawford tried to stop them firing by going through the form of the Benin salutation.

I can see the dear old man now standing some way in the bush, nodding his head like an old Chinese mandarin, and rubbing his hands slowly up and down. A silly lot of fools we must have looked in their eyes.

Mr. Powis was the most successful of us, as he could talk some of the Benin City language, and at first they seemed to want to let him alone. However, nothing we could do was of any good, so we tried using our sticks, with much more success. Although the Benin men, from all accounts, fought really pluckily against the Punitive Expedition a few weeks later, here they behaved like veritable curs, and ran away every time we charged them with our sticks. I fancy this was due to the bush being so thin that they wouldn't face us in the open.

It was hereabouts that I last saw Mr. Basilli, our Benin City guide. He was one of the crowd following us, and certainly was not wounded then. I saw him go up to one of the Benin City men who was shooting at us and say something in his ear, at which the Benin man nodded, but fired off his gun at us. We heard afterwards that Basilli had been wounded and taken prisoner, and also that he had told his people that if they opened any of our boxes they would all die, as there was a very powerful Juju in them. I doubt much whether Mr. Basilli ever said this, but suspect he got the message sent down to tell in his favour with the Protectorate authorities if he should ever come back again.

We all kept on charging into the bush whenever we saw any Benin men going to fire at us, and they invariably ran away. I came suddenly on one warrior who must have been chasing some of our wretched carriers into the bush on the other side, and collared his gun and machête. Our people set on him in a regular mob, but before we could do anything to him he managed to get away. The gun I gave to poor Baddoo, the chief clerk, and the machête to Herbert Clarke, the interpreter.

Soon after I came on one of our grave and reverend escort, one of the Benin messengers, shouting and yelling like a lunatic and waving a machête round his head. I chased him for all I was worth into the bush, and would have given a lot to be able to get my cane, a thin Neilgherry cane, and which would bend like a cutting whip, across his back, but he had too long legs and ran too fast for me.

All this time we were making our way along the road back to Gwatto, and no one had been badly hit except poor Elliot, who was bleeding badly from a wound in his head, round which he had wound his handkerchief. Most of us had been hit by small pellets, but none of the rest of us were damaged seriously. Though they fired a few rough round bullets, their favourite ammunition, as it is always in this part of West Africa, was what is called pot-leg, which is made by breaking up the small iron cooking-pots they get in trade into small jagged pieces. Poor old Crawford soon got a whole charge of pot-leg into his groin, and fell. As it was fired from a very short distance off, only about ten yards I think, the wound must have been a mortal one.

We picked the dear old man up and began

carrying him, though he told us he was done for, and implored us to leave him. He was perfectly calm and cool about it all the time, and seemed quite to expect that we should leave him behind, which of course was out of the question. Locke and Crawford's orderly, another civil policeman, carried him on the one side, Maling and myself on the other.

We, of course, had to go much slower now, so all our followers, servants, carriers, etc. went on in front of us with Mr. Powis. The last I saw of him was driving several Benin men, who had come out on the road, in front of him like a flock of sheep. From the very beginning they had seemed to recognise him, and appeared to be more unwilling to shoot him than the rest of us, and we hoped he might be allowed to get away; but, alas, no! for we heard from one of his own boys who escaped afterwards that he had seen his master lying dead on the road. Such a good chap he was too, and one of the most popular men at Old Calabar with everyone.

While we were carrying Crawford we suddenly heard the sound of a big drum being beaten somewhere or other in the bush. Although we knew perfectly well that it was only a drum, yet it sounded most mysterious and weird, the noise seeming to come from all parts of the bush at the same time. It was too much for Herbert Clarke, the interpreter, who had stopped behind with us, for as soon as he heard it he clapped his hands to his ears, saying, "My God, the war drum!" and bolted down the road as fast as he could to pick up the others. Just at this time, too, Locke heard a big gun go off far away down the road in front of us.

Dr. Elliot remained behind with us, and if any man ever deserved a V.C. he certainly did. As we could only go slowly, and afforded such a large mass to aim at, we gave the Benin men excellent chances for killing us all; but whenever he saw a man with a gun up, off would go Elliot into the bush and charge him out of it. If it hadn't been for his pluck and nerve, I am perfectly certain they would have killed us all at that time, for they would have had every opportunity of creeping up close to us and then firing at any or all of us. All the time, it must be remembered, he was bleeding profusely from the wound in his head.

How far we carried Crawford I don't know, perhaps a couple of hundred yards or so, but it seemed to me like a good mile. As we were going along I saw another Benin man behind a tree on the road exactly in front of us, and about fifteen yards off, aiming at us; so I told the others to put Crawford down on the bank while I charged the man out. As I was rushing at him I got another whole charge of pot-leg in the inside of my right arm, and fired by a man not much more than five yards off.

It was a piece of the most marvellous luck that it missed the bone of the arm and also my body, which it must have gone close to. If it had hit my body, it would have been in almost the same place poor Crawford was hit in, the left groin. The force of the blow was so great that it knocked me over like a shot rabbit.

However, the wound didn't hurt a bit, nor had it the slightest effect at the time on my arm, for I got up, picked up my cane in my right hand again, and chased the man from behind the tree before he had time to fire. He promptly ran away into the bush, so I went back to the others.

When I got there I found four out of the five of them dead and only Locke left alive, and he had a marvellous shave of it. Some of the Benin men had crept up behind them and shot them all in the back, and killed them all except poor Maling, who was just alive, and died in a few seconds. Crawford had been hit twice again, which made three big wounds altogether. Maling was hit twice, Elliot twice, and Crawford's orderly was also killed. Locke had been hit four times in the arm and once in the hip, but luckily none of the wounds was serious enough to stop him.

CHAPTER VII

OUR ESCAPE (*continued*)

BEING the only two left alive, and as the Benin men were now all round us, we decided to make a bolt into the bush towards the north, on the far side of the ambush, as we had realised by this time that it was hopeless to try and get to Gwatto back along the road we had come. Before leaving I told Locke to pick up the compass Maling had been using, for I had been told by some of the natives at Gwatto that the Gwatto Creek bent round to the right, eastward, after leaving that place, which would bring it nearer where we were. So we thought that by steering a course about N.W. we should reach the creek sooner. Also we did not want to go south, for that

OUR ESCAPE

would have brought us down towards Gwatto, and knowing, from what we had been told by Crawford and Maling, that Benin soldiers were always sent to guard all the waterside towns in the event of any excitement, we fancied there was likely to be less excitement higher up the creek, where it was more improbable any refugees would appear than farther down the Gwatto Creek, which was better known, nearer the limits of the Benin Country, and more likely for refugees to make for.

We were pretty well right too, especially about the distance, for from a survey of the creek done afterwards by Captain Burrows, it could not have been much more than seven miles from where we left the road. Of course we actually walked much more, perhaps seventeen miles altogether, but those seven miles took us five days to do.

Of course it is absolutely impossible to walk three yards in one direction in the bush unless one has a machête, or axe, or something to clear the way with; and as all our implements consisted of Locke's pocket-knife, we had to wander in all directions, though never backwards, if we could possibly avoid it.

I often wonder now how we managed to get through some of the places we did, some of which I can picture vividly to myself yet. They were places which looked as difficult to get through as a thick wall. However, one can do wonderful things to save one's own life, and we scrambled through, sometimes on hands and knees, sometimes at full length, dragging ourselves painfully along like sick worms. Sometimes when we came across a fallen tree, which made the bush clear up above, but a tremendous dense mass of undergrowth underneath, we managed to get along by jumping as far as possible into the middle of it, and getting out the other side as best we could. At other times, when we were very done and came to a particularly bad place, we would have a short rest first, and then tackle it.

It was always forward in a N.W. line as much as we could, or as near to N.W. as possible. Our worst times were on the edges

OUR ESCAPE

of plantations, for all the stuff that had been cleared to make the plantation was heaped together at the edge, and, with the bush already there, made an almost impenetrable black wall of undergrowth.

Then the thorns! when we eventually got out, there wasn't a space on any part of our heads or bodies as big as one's little finger free from those thorns.

The whole bush seemed to be full of thorns, for in addition to the palm-tree thorns, which were everywhere, there was a sweet creeper that straggled all over the place and had thorns like the barbs of a fish-hook. If it isn't called the "wait a bit" thorn, it ought to be, for it was useless going forward against it. One had to go backward and pick the thorns off like one would a fish-hook.

Locke had on, unfortunately for him, a pair of thin serge trousers, and when we eventually arrived at the waterside, those trousers were a picture. They were a mass of tears in every direction. The torn pieces were tied together with pieces of bush straw, and joined in other places with thorns: the poorest beggar that ever lived never had a more disreputable pair. I was luckier, as I had been walking in Khaki riding breeches, shooting boots, and gaiters, which saved me below the knee. Up above that I wasn't much better off than he was. To start with, my breeches had been cut across the right knee by a pellet, which had luckily only grazed the knee; and in addition to being torn, the right leg, after the third day, might have been made of corrugated iron instead of Khaki cloth, as it was perfectly stiff and hard from the blood that had come from my arm, which never stopped bleeding until it began to get rotten on the fourth day.

The thing that helped to our getting out at all was that there were two of us, both pretty hard and fit, for I don't believe one man by himself could have stood it, because thinking of all that he had left behind him, added to the apparent hopelessness of his position, would have been too much for any man's brain. With us we could help each other much, for when the leader arrived at some place he

OUR ESCAPE

considered almost hopeless, the other would take the lead in his turn.

However, to continue the story. It must have been between 3.30 p.m. and 3.45 p.m. when Locke and myself left the scene of the massacre. We ran down the path for a few yards, and then plunged into the north side of the bush, the general bearing of the road towards Benin City being a very little north of east. At first the bush was comparatively thin, so we could manage to run for a bit; but very soon it began to get thick, and this reduced our pace to a walk, and not a fast one either. At first we could hear the yells of the Benin men close behind us, as if they were following us; but if they were, they must have given it up pretty soon, as the yells began to get fainter and fainter, and I fancy each man was anxious to stop close to the road and get his share of the loot from our boxes. Every now and then we heard fresh volleys, with more yelling and squealing, which betokened that more of our wretched people had been discovered and murdered.

We went on some distance, but it is impossible to calculate distance even fairly accurately when one is going through the bush. But I should say in nearly two miles we came upon a plantation, which meant open ground, with every chance of being seen, and certain death if we were noticed. We thought at first of going round it, but soon settled to chance it, and run across the open as quick as we could. On the other side we met one of those black walls of undergrowth, and looked about for some gap or easy place to get through, but it all appeared much the same, so we simply charged the nearest point, and got through somehow or other with only the loss of my shirt, which, being a thin flannel, was torn to ribbons on my back and arms.

We went on through the bush as long as we could, but at last, about five o'clock, we sat down to rest, tired, hot and thirsty, for we had been going our best pace for about two hours. We had been sitting less than a minute when we suddenly heard two men talking to each other not twenty yards away from us. They appeared to be on the edge of another plantation, but fortunately there was another thick wall of undergrowth between us and them, and they were on slightly higher ground. Beyond a doubt, they were Benin men.

This was shock number one, and we had scarcely got accustomed to that when we got shock number two. This came from hearing a party of men cutting their way through the bush with machêtes from the direction in which we wanted to go, and coming, as we thought, straight for us. We shook hands with each other, saying "Good-bye, old chap," for we thought our turn had come, and envied all our poor friends lying dead on the road, for they had got over the worst of it.

One thing we determined was, not to be taken prisoners, but to make the brutes shoot us by trying to kill some of them, throttling them with our hands or anything we could do. However, to our intense relief, the party turned off at an angle and passed by us, some fifteen yards or so distant. We were crouching on the ground as low as we could, and could see about twenty men, all armed, some with boxes on their heads,—our boxes, of course,—cutting their way through the bush.

Our relief didn't last long, as we saw them leave one man, evidently a sentry, right opposite to us, and barely fifteen yards away. Luckily it was getting dark, and would soon be quite so, which gave us a better chance of getting off, for in broad daylight our white shirts must have been noticed at that distance off. When we had crouched down to avoid being seen, I had got into a most uncomfortable position, lying on my left side with all the weight of my body on my left elbow and my knees tucked well up, and I soon began to get cramp from it. I stood it as long as I could,—till long after dark, in fact,—and then tried to change my position. But each time I tried I felt a warning pinch on my boot from Locke to be quiet. He was far better off. He was lying full length on his chest, with a white pith solah topee under his chest, and his head supported by both elbows.

At last I couldn't stand the cramp any longer,

and shifted my position to a sitting one as quietly as I could. Quietly as I tried to do it, it seemed as if every twig and leaf within miles crackled. The sentry right in front of course heard me, and calling to another man on his right, and of whose presence we had been unaware up to then, they both began searching through the bush in the dark.

It wasn't pleasant sitting there listening to these men advancing through the bush for a few yards, then stopping for what seemed to us an interminable time to listen, then advancing again, and so on. At last they began to go back again in the same manner, and we breathed rather more freely when they stopped altogether. Our friend opposite, however, didn't seem to be quite satisfied, and made one or two more searches in the bush. Once he came so near us that we held our breath, expecting that the next second he was bound to step on to one or the other of us. Luckily he didn't, and went back as before, and after a bit he seemed satisfied and kept quiet.

Being now in a sitting position, with my

elbows on my knees, head on my elbows, and being very tired, I could not help dropping off to sleep, hard as I tried not to, and, much to Locke's annoyance (and my own too, for that matter), kept on waking up and saying something out loud. It was very annoying, and I really could not help it. Some time after this I wakened up, quietly this time, and felt a hand on my boot, then creeping up my gaiter. I thought it couldn't be Locke, who had been behind me, and must be of course a Benin man who had found us while I was sleeping. So I collared the hand and arm, intending to try and choke the man before he could give the alarm, but spoilt all this brilliant idea, and gave the alarm myself by yelling out in a loud tone, "Locke, I have got this brute!"

It turned out to be no brute of a Benin man, but Locke himself, who had shifted his position very quietly, and was trying to find out mine. Of course my shout was heard by the Benin men; and as we imagined trying to conceal ourselves further was useless, Locke suggested

OUR ESCAPE

we might as well try and have a decent sleep, which we did.

It must have been somewhere about four o'clock a.m. that we made out three men doing regular sentry-go round and round us. We could hear one man coming from a certain direction, and when he had got a certain distance round us there was a second, and eventually a third. I mean that we could hear three men walking round and round us.

We had given up all hopes of escaping long ago, so, being frightfully thirsty, we kept on calling to them for "oomi," water. "Oomi" is really a Yoruba word, but I believe the Benin City language is something like it, and there being many Yorubas trading regularly through the Benin Country, the people are bound to know words like "oomi." The men, however, took no notice of us, but kept on doing their round till nearly seven o'clock a.m., and long after daylight. Even in the light they kept so far away from us that we could not see them, and could only place them by the noise, and occasionally by seeing a piece of bush move.

Then by some miracle which I have never been able to account for to this day, they left us. Whether they thought we were dying and couldn't move, and so went off to get their food, expecting to find us there when they came back, or what was their reason for leaving, neither of us could guess. But leave us they did, which was the main point, and so ended the most awful day and night I have ever passed in my life.

At first we thought they had some sporting ideas about not shooting us while on the ground, but only when moving. So we remained some time after they had stopped walking round us. Hardly had they stopped when another man made his appearance, who turned out to be one of our runaway Jakri carriers, and belonging to Chief Dore. We spoke with him. He said he had seen no Benin men near us, and knew of no water, which was what we wanted most, but gave us a dry hard ship's biscuit each, which he had got as part of his rations, and which had been soaked in rank palm-oil to give it flavour.

We couldn't eat any of the biscuits in our thirsty state, and put them away in our pockets to be kept until we got to water. Mine unfortunately I put into my right-hand pocket, so it got soaked in blood also; and when I pulled it out four days afterwards at the waterside the smell of it was something awful. The carrier who had joined us preferred going on by himself to being accompanied by two clumsy white men with boots which made such a noise going through the bush; and very naturally too, for at that time there seemed to be many more chances in favour of his getting out safely than in ours. However, we did manage to escape, and he, poor beggar, did not, for we told Chief Dore about him, and he said that the man had never come back.

Soon after the carrier left, we started, quite expecting every second to hear shots ring out of the bush, for we fully thought that some of our Benin friends of the night before were still watching us from the bush, and would fire on us as soon as they saw us moving off. However, nothing happened, and we got away in the most absolutely miraculous manner.

We were frightfully thirsty, for we had had nothing to drink, not even dew, since 1 p.m. the day before; and as we thought we were close to the creek then, and might get there any minute, we never thought of sipping the dew that morning. Locke and myself were counting up afterwards, and found that we had been forty-one hours without even a drop of dew to quench our horrible thirst. Another thing which disappointed us badly and frequently at first, and until we became weaker and more callous, I suppose, was that we kept on thinking that we had at last reached the creek. As one comes through the bush and approaches a plantation, one sees over the top of the bush, all the tall trees suddenly ending. Then will come a gap, then the tall trees beginning again; and each time we came to a place like this, we fondly imagined we had at last reached the creek and water. Many and bitter were our disappointments in consequence. Immediately after we had left our sleeping-place, we came on the track which we had seen and heard the Benin men cutting the evening before. Unfortunately it was of no use to us, as it led in the wrong direction. So bang into the thick bush we had to go again, trying to keep our direction as much as possible. With a few short halts we struggled on to 11.30 a.m. or so, and then lay down and had a real good sleep till about 3 p.m., when we went on again. We came on one of the Benin men's roads a little before dusk, and followed it for some distance, until we fancied we were coming close to a village. We then struck off into the bush once more, and lay down for the night amidst the roots of a large tree, about twenty yards away from the road. Hardly had we sat down when we heard two somethings or somebodies moving about the bush near us, which was no imagination; and close behind me I could detect distinctly the smell of a native who had been eating strong meat, which was also no imagination, for there is no mistaking that smell when one has once experienced it.

After that Locke saw two men near him, and I saw, or thought I saw, most distinctly, a little old man sitting down about a couple of yards away from Locke, and looking at us hard. This little old man corresponded exactly with one of the men Locke saw; but as they vanished most mysteriously and silently some time afterwards, we put our visions down to imagination, which most probably they were. However, before the little old man vanished, we kept up, or tried to keep up, a most animated conversation with him, in which of course the principal word was "oomi," water, and we offered him several most valuable articles, such as Locke's tie, pocket-knife, etc. etc., if he would only bring us some water.

However, real or unreal, the little old man never said a word to us, nor did he produce any water. While we were in the middle of this conversation with him, we heard a man and a child talking to each other as they went along the road. To him we also called out "Oomi, oomi." He at anyrate was a reality, for he answered back at once, "Oomi nahun," or some word like it, which we took to mean that he could give us no water; after this our old gentleman vanished.

As it was cold at night, Locke, who was the lucky possessor of a shirt and singlet, lent me the latter, as my shirt had been torn to ribbons the day before. However, the shirt came in useful after all, part of it acting as a bandage for my arm, and the rest of it as a pillow by night, and a turban by day, when we were exposed to the sun in plantations and such-like. I had left my hat, shot off by a pellet, at the scene of the massacre.

It was so cold at night that I used to spread a small silk handkerchief I had over my chest, fold my arms underneath it, and try to imagine it was a sheet. Perhaps, thanks to a powerful imagination, I felt a bit warmer after it.

We slept fairly well that night under the big tree. About 6 a.m. on the 6th January we got our first sip of dew, and the first moisture—one can't call it drink—we had had since before one o'clock p.m. two days previously, forty-one hours in all. At first we were very ignorant beginners at this kind of drink, but by the time we got to the water we were quite connoisseurs, knew which leaves held the biggest drops, how to circumvent those big drops, and so on, and so on. However, the dew wasn't very satisfying, as even on our best day, if we had been able to collect all the dew we drank, I don't suppose it would have amounted to more than a tablespoonful. If we could feel even a small drop of liquid trickling down our throats, we considered ourselves lucky, for as a rule the drops we drank, or rather sipped, were only enough to moisten the tongue and perhaps the back of the throat. All this sounds very exaggerated, but it is so in no way at all.

Soon after starting we got into a plantation, and did better in the dew line, for the big plantain leaves held many more and much bigger drops of dew than any of the bush plants. Plantains were the only fruit we came across, except a sort of wild cherry, which was of no use, for, in addition to our being uncertain about it being poisonous, it had no moisture inside. The plantains also were useless to us, for they were unripe, bitter and quite dry, so that with our parched throats we were quite unable to swallow them.

We never came across any fruit we wanted to find, such as bananas, pine-apples, or papaws, and we were unfortunately too ignorant to make use of any roots or such-like that might have done us some good. Having nothing but dew to drink, we used to pray for a shower of rain every night, so that we could take off our boots and get them filled, and have a real fair and square drink. But luckily for us no rain came, for if we had been drenched in addition to all our other woes, we would have been certain to have had a bad go of fever when we got down to Benin River, if not before.

CHAPTER VIII

OUR ESCAPE (*continued*)

THE story of this and the following day, the 7th, is much the same. It was one continual hard struggle through the bush, our bodies getting weaker each day and more torn, and more and more in want of water. Occasionally we found paths through the bush which are called hunters' paths, and which are merely tracks through the bush, but they were joy to us when they led us in the direction we wanted to go for some distance; but as a rule they went the wrong way, and back again we would have to go into that wretched bush.

Although sometimes very close to people and villages, we met no more men face to face. On the third day of our escape, Locke lost the big compass out of his pocket, and we had to rely on a very small, almost toy compass I had fastened on to my watch chain. By the way, I kept that watch, a small gun-metal one, wound up and going the whole time, so that, even if we had had no compass, we could have guessed our way fairly well by the time of day and the direction of the sun.

We kept on wondering when, if ever, we were going to reach the water; and although we knew that by keeping on in the same direction we must get to the Gwatto Creek some time or other, after this continual struggle we began to feel a bit hopeless. If we were moving, we were so tired we wanted to be resting; if we were resting, we wanted to be moving, as we couldn't get to the waterside by resting. If we were asleep, we wanted to be awake, to escape the visions of numberless long drinks we were just on the point of drinking, but never succeeded in getting hold of; and if we were awake, we wanted to be asleep, to escape the horrible thoughts of all our dear old pals left murdered on the roadside.

The only hours we looked forward to at all were from six o'clock to ten o'clock a.m., which were the dew times. For after that all dew had disappeared. Luckily we both slept well, and above all we both started pretty hard and fit, for if one of us had got seedy, neither of us would have escaped.

Luckily, too, for me, I couldn't have had a better or pluckier companion than Locke. Always cheery, never beaten, and (to use a very vulgar expression) always with his tail up, he was always ready to get along somehow or somewhere, when I couldn't see any possible means of pushing farther. He had been out about thirteen months in the country already, myself not six, yet it wasn't until our last day in the bush that he began to show any signs of our hard work telling on him, and that, I fancy, was mostly my fault, or rather my arm's fault. It had begun to get bad then, and smelt so much that it made Locke very nearly sick, and forced him to get away as far from me as he could, and made me wish I could get away the same distance from it.

To continue. We were unlucky on Friday the 8th in not getting so much dew as usual, as we did not find a plantation till about 10 a.m., when most of the dew had disappeared. However, I discovered that each of the plantain branches had a small reservoir of dew mixed with ants and dirt, though that didn't matter as long as we got the liquid. We had to tread carefully in this plantation, as we had seen an old woman at the other end of it, and also had heard people talking not far away, and it was only after a good deal of trouble that about 10.30 a.m. we found a good place to lie down in.

We were both frightfully tired and done up, and personally I believe I was asleep before my head touched the ground. We slept on and off till about 3.30 p.m., when I suggested to Locke that it was time for us to be on the tramp again. He said, "Oh, let's stop here for the night,"—a proposition I was only too ready to agree to, being so tired. Here again our marvellous luck, or rather more than luck, showed itself, for if we had gone on that afternoon we must have struck the waterside before dark and found Benin soldiers waiting for us.

By this time my wound had got very bad, and was oozing with a kind of red mud. Locke had made his holes healthier by employing his spare time in squeezing them dry, but the holes in my arm were too big to do the same to. Part of the charge had come out on the other side of my arm, but the biggest hole was on the inside, where the whole charge had gone in. The ubiquitous flies evidently thought I was carrion, for they appeared as if by magic and settled in hundreds on the shirt round my arm, which smelt so much now that poor old Locke was nearly made sick by it, and had to get as far away from me as our shelter would allow.

Several times during the day I had noticed kingfishers flying about, which made me hope we were getting near water at last, and before night came on we were attacked by swarms of a brand of mosquito I have never seen before,— and I know a good many types of that furious animal. These were little red furry beggars, and regular tigers for blood. What with the

OUR ESCAPE

mosquitoes, and the long sleep we had had in the middle of the day, neither of us had a second's sleep that night. Most of my time was employed in taking off the ooze, that was coming out of my arm, with big leaves, for it was coming out faster and the arm was getting worse every hour; and towards morning the stuff was coming out as fast as I could scrape it off. We had recognised a long time ago that we were within a quarter of a mile of a village, and we were getting so thirsty and done up that we very nearly settled to go straight in, ask for water, and take our chance of being shot. Thank God, we didn't, but decided to give the Gwatto Creek another day before we tried the mercy of the Benin men.

We were up trying to sip dew long before daylight the next morning, but it hadn't fallen properly by then, so we had to sit and wait. My arm by this time was perfectly loathsome, and anyone could easily have tracked us by the droppings off it. We had our best drink of dew that morning, for having slept in the plantation we were ready on the spot, and had great times as we worked our way across it.

We had to keep to one side a good deal, the side nearest to the village, as we saw smoke coming from the opposite end of the plantation. When we got across the plantation to the bush on the other side, we saw that the ground suddenly sloped down at a very steep angle, and if we had not been so dry, in spite of our "big drink" of dew, I believe we would have yelled with delight, for it meant that at last we were really near water.

We must have gone down nearly two hundred feet before we reached a small dry creek at the bottom; and when I say dry, I mean not running. But to our intense joy there was a small pool of water close to where we reached the bottom. It had evidently been scooped out, and was used by the people of the village near, which we had been so close to the previous night.

However, all we cared about at that moment was that there was a real good honest drink at last. I was first down the hill, and so first at the waterside, poor old Locke growling away that it was his turn long before I was nearly ready to stop drinking. How we enjoyed that drink too! The creek, like all the little ones that run into the Gwatto Creek, was so far dry at this season that there was no running water, but water is obtained by the Benin people by digging small pools like the one we had been drinking at.

We knew now that we must be close to the Gwatto Creek, and that this little one would lead us into it. So we tried to follow it down, but had to give that up pretty soon, as it was all overgrown with bush. So we climbed up the bank again, and found a path which led in the proper direction.

After about a quarter of a mile we saw some huts in front. We knew well enough it was risky work entering a village, for we expected that at all the waterside villages there would be Benin soldiers watching for us; but we had settled to chance it, and, if they produced their guns, to make a rush for the waterside and try and swim over to the other bank, where we should be comparatively safe, it being part of the

Benin men's Juju not to get into a canoe and cross water.

Consequently we walked straight on into the village, which consisted only of about four or five huts, and we met four men, all unarmed. They turned out to be Jakris from a bigger trading village on the opposite side of the creek, and were on this side for the purpose of taking any trade-stuff the Benin people brought down; but of course we didn't know this at the time. We promptly began our old cry of "Oomi, oomi," but, instead of giving us any water, they hurried us away towards the stream, two of them running on in front and getting a small dugout of a canoe ready.

There was a small creek here, which, after turning a corner, led us into the Gwatto Creek. As soon as we had got into the canoe, the two men paddled hard until we were round a corner, and then stopped and let us have another drink. Lovely clear light green water flowing above a sandy bottom. As soon as we had got into the canoe, I let my wretched arm trail along in the water, the first wash it had had since I was hit;

and when the canoe stopped for us to drink, poor old Locke first of all put his head over on the same side as my arm, but very soon altered to the other side, as he had had about enough of it by this time.

When we had drank our fill, which took some time, our two friendly paddlers went on and took us across the Gwatto Creek to a larger village of about twenty-five or thirty huts, which was called Aketti, and was inhabited by Jakris. Here Locke recognised and was recognised by the head man, who had traded to Warri, the Vice-Consulate of Locke's district; and so now we knew that we were more or less safe. They told us here that the reason the men had hurried us out so quick from the small village opposite, was because there were some Benin soldiers living there, watching for refugees, and these had left the village only about twenty minutes before we arrived, to get yams for their breakfast. If we had arrived at this village on the afternoon before, as we certainly should have done if we hadn't been too tired to go on, or in fact if we had arrived at almost any other time except when we did, these Benin men would have shot us, or done their best to, for a certainty. So here was more marvellous good luck.

Of course our arrival at Aketti created a tremendous excitement; for the people there had been told that all the white men had been killed, and certainly never expected to see any of them nearly five days after the massacre. The head man said he would get a canoe ready to take us away, and while he was doing so he asked us to sit behind some huts, so that we shouldn't be seen from the opposite side, in case any Benin men were watching. He also produced some excellent palm-wine for us, which is very good while quite fresh, but beastly afterwards, I think, though the natives prefer it sour and potent.

We sat down behind the huts, and were the objects of much interest to the inhabitants, both male and female, of the village. But as two specimens of the ruling race, we couldn't have been much of a success, for there couldn't have been found two more miserable-looking objects. We were unshaven and unwashed; our bodies were bloody; our clothes all torn and dirty; not a square inch of our bodies that wasn't black with thorns. We must have been two miserable-looking specimens of humanity.

The first thing we did after having had a drink was to light cigarettes. I had a case full of Egyptians in my pocket, and wanted often to smoke one in the bush; but what with Locke stopping me, and also the idea that it would make my mouth still drier than it was, if possible, I hadn't done so. My possessions in my pocket consisted of a box of wooden matches, pipe, watch, which I had kept going regularly, the small compass which we had used for the last two days, and two lucky coins fastened on to the ring of the watch. Locke had lost most of his possessions, as he had trousers on with side pockets.

We could get little or no information out of the Aketti people. All they could tell us was that they had heard that all the white men had been killed, and that none except ourselves had escaped so far. Although they were more or less safe on this side of the creek, they were packing up their belongings and preparing to leave the place, as they knew there would be a big war palaver soon, and were frightened at the Benin men shooting at them across the creek, which was about forty yards wide there.

While our canoe was being got ready, we heard an old hag screaming and yelling, "fit to bust herself," as the small Cockney would say, and we were told at the time that one of her sons was to be one of our paddlers, and she was frightened that he might be shot by the Benin men as we went down the creek. We thought this didn't sound very probable, but it was the only answer we could get at the time, and were not told till we were safe out of the country that the old hag was a Benin woman sent across to Aketti as a spy, and that she was yelling to her people across the creek to come and shoot two white men who were escaping. Old brute! If we had known, I think we would have had her smuggled into the canoe and brought her away as a curiosity.

We wanted to go and hurry up the canoe which was being got ready for us, but our head man implored us not to come down to the bank, for he said the Benin men had sentries posted all down the opposite bank, and if they were to see us they would shoot at the canoe.

After what seemed to us a very long time, we were told that the canoe was ready, and we lay down at full length in the middle of it, having mats placed over us to hide us from the Benin men. I was on the Benin side, and could see several places down by the water's edge, where our head man told us the Benin sentries were on the watch; but I saw no man.

We had struck the water about eighteen miles above Gwatto, so it wasn't till about three o'clock that our head man said we were out of the Benin Country, and took off the mats. It had been awfully hot underneath them in the blaze of the sun, and I was most thankful for the remnants of my shirt to act as a turban. Dear old Locke's liver had got out of order, and most of the way down he kept worrying to have the mats removed, and I only pacified him by saying that, after all we had gone through, it wasn't good enough to run the risk of being shot at again when we were so nearly safe.

On the way down, and before passing Gwatto, we met our former messenger to Benin going back to Aketti to collect his goods and chattels. In fact, all the Jakris and Ejaws trading up this creek came away in the course of the next week or so, for they knew it must lead to a big expedition against the Benin City men, which meant for them no more chance of any trade, only that of being shot at across the creek by the Beninis. Our former messenger, poor chap, was nearly as big a wreck as ourselves, and he told me that he had also had to run for his life, after taking Phillips' last message to the King.

We didn't pass Gwatto itself, as there was another passage which missed it; and soon after leaving Gilli Gilli we had the mats off, and could breathe more freely, for we were perfectly safe then. Though scarcely fit enough to realise all that that meant, it was a most blessed relief to think that we should have no more crawling about the bush, and no necessity to

OUR ESCAPE

look for dew. There was always that dreadful thought, though: "If only we could have had our other dear old pals with us."

As soon as our mats were off, the head man produced some "fu-fu" he had made for us, and very readily we ate it. That was the first food we had had for over five days. Fu-fu is made either from yams or plantains, the latter, in this case, by pounding them up until they resemble dough. He also produced a demijohn, a big trade-bottle, covered with straw, and generally used in trade for rum. It was filled with fresh palm-wine, of which we had already had a taste at Aketti.

After this came more relief in taking off our boots and socks and bathing our feet. My boots hadn't been off all these five days, and, as they were old shooting boots, they had got wrinkled up and cut into my instep. All this time, too, my arm was trailing along in the water, which washed out all the filth. When the wound was clean it showed things like the broken ends of lamp-wick,—ligatures, I believe, which had been shot through,—and the hole was big enough to put two fingers in at one time up to the first joint. On the other side was a smaller hole, out of which part of the charge had passed. Locke's wounds, whether owing to their being smaller ones, or to his having squeezed them so much, were in a much healthier condition. The worst he had was on his leg; it had been originally caused by a thorn, and aggravated by coming suddenly on some of the remaining nails of my boot when I was entangled and trying to struggle out of a lot of creepers. This wound gave him no end of trouble afterwards, as it festered and had to be cut open two or three times, and never got really well till he arrived home in England.

By the way, one of the men who was paddling our canoe had been one of the carriers on our ill-fated expedition, but could tell us no fresh news whatever. All he knew was that he suddenly heard a lot of shots fired, and saw several carriers fall, so promptly chucked his load down, and ran away into the bush. He arrived at Aketti two or three days before us.

As there was not time for us to get either to

OUR ESCAPE

Sapele or New Benin, *i.e.* any of the factories on the Benin River, before dark, we settled to go and stop for the night with Chief Dudu, about the next most powerful Jakri chief to Chief Dore. I have already mentioned that his town was situated up a small creek near the Benin River, and we intended sleeping at his house, and getting him to send, what is called in those parts, a despatch canoe, to Sapele, where we imagined everyone was still, to let them know that we had escaped, and wanted a steam launch to come and fetch us. However, it was very slow work in a canoe with only five paddlers, and they were getting a bit tired out at the end.

On the way down we met any amount of canoes going up, nearly all of them being Jakri or Ejaw canoes going up to fetch all their belongings. Amongst other canoes we met one of Herbert Clarke's, whose boys were going up to try and find out what had become of him. We could only tell them what had happened, and that we didn't know whether he was alive or dead.

At last, just before dusk, we got into the same reach that Chief Dudu's creek branched out of, and were nearly there, when we suddenly saw one of our own Protectorate launches come round the corner, and drop anchor just off the creek. Our feelings can scarcely be imagined, and I think both of us felt a bit mad at the sight.

We were very frightened that the launch might only have a message for Chief Dudu, and might up anchor and be off before we could get there, for we were still some three hundred yards away, and they weren't likely to take much notice of a small canoe like ours. However, we made the men paddle like demons, and I seized the remains of Locke's sun hat, intending to stand up and wave it. Locke vowed I would upset the canoe, so we made the head man stand up and wave it for all he was worth.

Very soon we could see our signals answered by handkerchiefs being waved from the bows of the launch, and as we got close we made out a group of two white men and six or seven black ones crowded on the bows, waving, yelling, and cheering like anything. The two white men turned out to be Lyon, one of our Assistant District Commissioners, and Mr. Swainson, Mr. Pinnock's agent, both of whom I have mentioned before. They told us afterwards that their attention was first drawn to the canoe by seeing the hat waving, and that very soon, though they could scarcely believe their eyes, they made out two white men. They had given up hope at least two days before of any white men escaping, and looked on us more as ghosts than anything else at first. I don't think they will mind my saying that they were both crying with joy at seeing us when our canoe got down to the launch.

It was a very choky time for all of us.

CHAPTER IX

OUR ESCAPE (*continued*)

AS we drew up to the launch, of course they wanted to help us into it. Locke was the first, but as soon as they touched him he yelled out that we weren't to be touched, being such a mess of thorns and prickles and wounds. They both said afterwards they had never seen two such miserable-looking scarecrows before. Having got us into the launch, and told our rescuer, the head man, where to come to, to get the "dash" we had promised him, we went off full speed ahead for New Benin, where we were told everybody had gone down to from Sapele.

I won't try and describe our feelings at finding ourselves once more on one of our own

OUR ESCAPE

launches, and away from all the horrors we had gone through. As we started, a bottle of champagne was produced, and a glass of it given to us. Another Gold Coast man, Quartey by name, was cook of the launch, and no one seemed more pleased to see us than he was. He kept standing at the entrance of the cabin, staring at us, and on every possible occasion produced the following : " God save Her Majesty the Queen, and to hell" (please forgive the language) "with Abu Binni, the King of Benin."

After we had finished our champagne, we were allowed a whisky and soda, and soon after a cocktail, by which time a plate of most excellent soup had been got ready for us, which we drank greedily, accompanied by more champagne. If ever we ought to have been intoxicated, it was that night, but strange to relate we were not, nor did we suffer any evil effects afterwards from our libations.

It got dark before we got to New Benin, but as we passed each factory Lyon yelled out that Locke and myself had escaped, and both white and black men turned out and cheered till long after we had passed.

It was a veritable resurrection from the dead. We were to stop at the African Association's factory, which was next the old Consulate here. There was a company of my black troops here, and when they heard the commandant had escaped, and arrived back, they turned out in a mass on to the boat pier, which they broke down by their weight, with the intention of carrying us up to the house. It was only after a lot of pain, and by using what little physical force we had left, that we were able to make them understand that we were too sore to be carried, and preferred walking.

Our doctor, D'Arcy Irvine, was dining on the Niger Company steamer *Nupe*, which Mr. Flint of the Niger Company had most kindly brought Captain Burrows round in from the Forcados River. Captain Burrows of the L. N. L. Regiment had been in the Niger Coast Protectorate Force, but had been appointed District Commissioner of the Benin and Sapele District, and had just come out after his leave home.

He was in the mail steamer in the Forcados River when the first news of the disaster came down from Warri, and it was owing to Mr. Flint's kindness in bringing him round on the *Nupe* that he was able to get round so soon.

As soon as D'Arcy Irvine heard of our arrival, he hurried over, put us into a carbolic bath, to try and get a little of the dirt off us, and packed us off to bed as soon as possible, after having dressed our wounds. Personally, I can just remember the satisfaction of feeling a bed beneath me once more, and dozing off at once, and feeling very badly treated when I was wakened up to take some meat extract or something of that sort. And so ended one of the very luckiest days of my life.

I was up at 6.30 a.m. next morning,—and oh, the relief of waking up and finding a roof over one's head! — after a lovely sleep, and went to tell Locke to hurry up, as there was a grand collection of dew on the verandah outside. It was most unfortunate that the Protectorate yacht *Ivy* should have left the Benin River only the morning before, and that we should have missed her by so few hours, for it would have saved our relatives four terrible days of anxiety, during which they thought we were killed like all the other poor fellows. All communications from Benin and Sapele to England or any of the cable stations—Brass, Bonny, or Lagos—have to go to the Forcados River, and thence on by the first steamer leaving. The *Axim*, the mail steamer that Captain Burrows came out in, was lying in Forcados River when the first terrible news of the massacre came down *viâ* Sapele and Warri. She promptly went off to Brass, and sent the news from there, while the yacht *Ivy* went to Bonny, and cabled from there to England. After this no steamer left Forcados River for four days, and consequently our telegram announcing our escape didn't arrive in England till four days after the first news. Such awful days they were, too, to our nearest and dearest! How I wish that more of our party, if not all, could have also been able to cable home their safety.

Burrows came to see us the first thing in

the morning, and immediately sent more canoes up the Gwatto Creek to try and pick up any more possible survivors. There had been several canoes sent up before. The next day he himself started up, in one of the launches, to see if he could do any good by using the steam-launch whistle to let any survivors know that friends were near. Captain Cockburn, an officer of the Queen's Bays, and attached to the Protectorate Force, who was surveying and sounding the Gwatto Creek, also went up several times.

However, altogether in the end only about fifteen Kroo boys and about forty Jakris escaped, and none of the Gold Coast men. The rest must have been killed or taken prisoners.

Early in the morning our Chief Tormentor, as we used to call Dr. D'Arcy Irvine, dressed our wounds, and it was then that he told me that another day in the bush without water would have made my arm mortify, and he doubted whether it would have been possible then to have saved my life. Though we called him our Chief Tormentor in fun, we were exceedingly lucky in having such a man as D'Arcy Irvine to look after us, for we couldn't possibly have had anyone more skilful or more delicate in the way he treated us.

The dressing time for our wounds was generally in the afternoon; and it was rather an amusing one, for when Irvine called out for first patient, we each of us tried to get the other taken first. However, the one who was dressed and bandaged first scored in the end, as he used to go and jeer at No. 2, when his turn came.

At first my wound hurt a good deal, the probe, by the way, being able to go through both holes and stick out each side of the arm; but very soon, thanks to D'Arcy's wonderful treatment and care, it began to heal in the most marvellous fashion, and was very nearly entirely closed up in three weeks. D'Arcy Irvine had of course probed it to see if any of the charge was left in the arm, but found none. Locke's worst wound was on his leg, caused by a thorn, and aggravated by the nails of my

OUR ESCAPE

shooting boot. It kept on getting bad and having to be cut open again.

During the next three weeks we got very little news. Captain Gallwey, now Acting Consul-General, came round in H.M.S. *Widgeon*, and we heard that the Punitive Expedition was to be a very big naval one. We also heard that our chief, Mr. Moor, had left England for Benin, with most of the Protectorate officers who were home on leave; but that was about all. During this time Burrows and Lyon had been very busy surveying and reconnoitring all the creeks round the Benin Country, and getting all the information they could. One message was sent up to the King of Benin asking if any white men were still alive. The answer was "None," and as a proof of it he sent back two rings that had belonged to poor old Crawford. I never heard the other gruesome story about poor Mr. Gordon's finger and rings, until I saw it in the English papers on my way homewards. We sent up another message soon after, asking again if any white men were alive, and got down an answer from the King to the effect that there were no white men alive in Benin City, and that he (the King) would receive no more messages from the white men. If they wanted to come and fight, let them come. He would send down soldiers to the waterside to fight the white men. If these were killed, he would send down more until all his soldiers were killed; and then he would run away. "His Majesty" acted up to his words, too.

About the 28th or 29th January, Locke was fit enough to go back to Warri, his station, where he was going to wait for a homeward boat. Having been out already fourteen months, he was a month overdue for leave. Anyway, he would have had to go home on sick leave, as his leg would have prevented him joining the Punitive Expedition.

I was ordered home too, but, feeling nearly all right again, I thought I would stop out and try and go on the Punitive Expedition. Meanwhile, as I had next to no kit, I thought I might get to Old Calabar and back in time for the expedition, and bring back some of my kit that I had left behind there. So I went

OUR ESCAPE

down to Forcados with Locke, and got on board the S.S. *Bonny*, one of the Old Calabar mail boats. She was discharging cargo for Lagos, so couldn't leave for two days. Meanwhile H.M.S. *Alecto* came in, and the officers told me that the Punitive Expedition was to start from Sapele about the 12th February.

This wouldn't have given me time to get to Old Calabar and back in time, and as poor Captain Pritchard, who was killed afterwards, kindly offered to take me back to New Benin, back again I went.

After stopping at New Benin for three or four days, we all went to Sapele to wait for the Punitive Expedition, the main column of which was to start from a place called Warrigi, a few miles below Sapele. There we found H.M.S. *Phœbe*. The Niger Coast Protectorate Force and most of the carriers arrived about 4th February, the former marching straight on to a place called Ciri, about seven miles off, and situated on the Ilogi Creek. About one mile farther up the creek, on the Benin side, is Ilogbo, a Benin town, from which Benin City was supposed to be only about twelve miles distant. It was along this road, which was an extremely bad one, being very narrow, with thick bush nearly all the way, that the main column were to go. The Niger Coast Protectorate Force, as soon as they arrived at Ciri, were set to work making a broad road back to Warrigi, while as many carriers as could be spared began at Warrigi, the bluejackets making the necessary bridges, one of the *St. George's* being indeed a work of art.

The Naval Brigade were taken from the *St. George*, Admiral Rawson's flagship, *Theseus*, *Forte* (these three being too big to come through the creek, remained about twenty miles out at sea from Forcados, with the *Malacca*, the hospital ship), the *Philomel*, *Barrosa*, and *Widgeon*, which formed the Gwatto column, and the *Phœbe*, *Magpie*, and *Alecto*, which formed the Jamieson River column. Several special service officers had come out to join the force for the expedition, among them being Colonel Bruce Hamilton of the East Yorkshire Regiment, in command, and Major Langdon of

OUR ESCAPE

the Army Service Corps as second in command; so that, although actually commandant of the Niger Coast Protectorate Force, I should have had to act as a company officer if I had been able to go up with the expedition.

As we had all been reported killed, Mr. Moor had applied to the War Office for two senior officers to command the Force, and the news of my safety only reached home the day before Mr. Moor and all the special service officers left England for the expedition, too late to make any change. Even then they didn't think I would be fit enough to go up with this expedition, which eventually turned out to be the case, as after arriving at Ciri on the 9th February and stopping there three days, I was ordered home on sick leave, neither nerves nor physical condition being in a fit enough state to allow me to go on with the expedition. It was very hard luck, for I wanted to go up badly, if it was only to have some revenge for the murder of so many dear friends.

Thus I can give no eye-witness account of

the doings of the Punitive Expedition; but from the accounts of those who went up, the state of Benin City when they got in there on the 18th February was something too awful. The remains of hundreds of human sacrifices were everywhere. Some were still on the crucifixion trees, others lay in deep pits all over the city, but especially were there crowds close to the King's Compound. And these, together with others in a large open space, where there were thousands of dead bodies in all stages of decomposition, mixed with skeletons from former "customs," made such a terrible effluvium that nearly all the officers and men suffered badly from nausea when they first arrived in the city.

The pits were about as bad as anything to look upon, for in them living, dead, and dying were thrown indiscriminately. It is a great pity that the governors of Benin City, or the head Juju men, escaped, for there is not much doubt that it was they who were responsible for our massacre, and for all the abominations that went on in the city.

OUR ESCAPE

The King himself, according to native accounts, had not nearly so much to say towards it, and was more or less a figure-head. He was supposed to be the impersonation of the Juju or religion of the country, and was in consequence never allowed to leave the Compound, and only to be seen by his people once a year. The mere fact of his having had to run away and leave Benin City ought to destroy to a great extent the belief of the natives in the power of their Juju.

I left Ciri on the 12th, and started down from Warrigi in a small German branch steamer hired from Lagos the same day. The next day I was caught up by another branch boat, the *Ilorin*, with Captain Koe of the Force, who had been wounded in the right arm during the first twenty minutes' fighting at Ologbo, and was also going home on sick leave, as the bone in his arm had been shattered. The *Ilorin* took us both out to the hospital ship *Malacca*, where we spent two days until the 16th February, when the S.S. *Bonny* came and took us on, arriving at Liverpool on the 16th March.

The doctors who said I would break down if I went on with the expedition were perfectly correct, for I more or less did so when I got on board the *Bonny*, and, writing this account now, nearly two months after I arrived home, am still suffering from the effects of all we went through.

CHAPTER X

THE PUNITIVE EXPEDITION

AS soon as the news of the massacre of our expedition arrived at home, *i.e.* on the 11th January, telegrams were sent at once to Admiral Rawson, C.B., commanding the Naval Squadron at the Cape, to organise a Punitive Expedition as soon as possible, the expedition, of course, being almost entirely a naval one, with the assistance of the Niger Coast Protectorate Force. This expedition took Benin City on the 18th February,—only about five weeks after the first telegrams. Marvellously smart work, especially when one considers the distances most of the expedition had to come, the extraordinary arrangements that had to be made for it in the shape of carriers from all parts of West Africa (between three and four thousand being employed), stores, etc. etc., and last, but not least, the nature of the country through which they had to fight their way.

As I have said before, the naval force was taken from H.M. Ships *Theseus, Forte, St. George, Phœbe, Philomel, Barrosa, Widgeon, Magpie,* and *Alecto,* whilst an additional force of marines was sent out in the P. & O. S.S. *Malacca,* which was to act as, and had been fitted up as hospital ship. The first two ships, H.M.S. *Theseus* and *Forte,* came from the Mediterranean Squadron, while the remainder belonged to the Cape Squadron. As I have already mentioned, the *Theseus, Forte,* and *St. George* being too large to come over the bar of the Forcados River, anchored off its mouth, but the rest came up the Benin River through the Forcados River and Nanna Creek.

The main column was to advance on Benin City by what is called the Ilogbo route,—Ilogbo being a Benin village on the Ilogi Creek and supposed to be only about twelve or fourteen

THE PUNITIVE EXPEDITION 169

miles from Benin City. The distance turned out to be about twenty-two miles. The Ilogi Creek is the creek from which the Benin City people used to get their water, and at that place was called the Ikpoba Creek. Unfortunately for the expedition, it soon got too shallow and full of snags and obstructions to allow of any steam-launches or boats going up it, and being of any use to the marching column.

To reach Ilogbo the force landed at a place called Warrigi, a few miles below Sapele on the Benin River, and marched about seven miles across to Ciri, a friendly village on one side of the Ilogi Creek and about one mile below Ilogbo. When the advance began it had been the Admiral's intention to throw a wire suspension bridge across the Ilogi Creek, but unfortunately the bridge could not be used owing to swamps. The Protectorate troops arrived at Ciri about the 4th of February, and started cutting a road back to Warrigi, while a party of carriers, with the help of some bluejackets, began the road from the other end, and a very good road was ready for the Admiral's inspection when he came to visit Ciri on the 9th February.

Meanwhile there was a lot of work going on at Warrigi organising the great number of carriers that were to accompany the expedition. These men came from Sierra Leone and the Gold Coast, and some, of course, were supplied by the Jakri Chiefs of the Benin River, and belonged to many and various tribes of West Africa. In addition there was a force of some hundred or more scouts raised in Lagos by Mr. Turner, a travelling commissioner of the Niger Coast Protectorate, and officered by him and Lieutenant Erskine, R.N. They looked a very brave sight in red shirts and fezes, and I believe did very fairly well afterwards, especially considering that it had only been possible to give them a very few days' drill.

On the 10th February the remainder of the bluejackets and marines forming the main column landed at Warrigi, and marched across to Ciri the next day, so that the advance on Benin City began on the 12th February. The Protectorate Force was under the command of

THE PUNITIVE EXPEDITION 171

Lieutenant - Colonel Bruce Hamilton of the East Yorkshire Regiment, who had been sent out by the War Office with the following special service officers, Major Langdon, A.S.C., as second in command, Captains Walker, Scottish Rifles, and O'Shee, R.E. The officers actually belonging to the Force present were Major Searle, the permanent second in command, Captains Ringer Koe, late of the Royal Irish, Carter of the Black Watch, Lieutenant Cockburn of the Queen's Bays, and Lieutenant Daniels, a native officer, and as plucky as any white man.

Before the main column advanced two flanking columns had been sent by the Admiral for the purpose of drawing away the enemy's attention from the main attack, and also to try and stop any fugitives escaping from Benin City. Unfortunately they were not successful in stopping the King and his Juju men when they fled. One of these columns went up the Jamieson River under the command of Captain M'Gill, R.N., and the other, under Captain O'Callaghan, R.N., went up the Gwatto Creek.

Captain M'Gill's force, which was made up from men of the *Phœbe*, *Magpie*, and *Alecto*, proceeded up the Jamieson River as far as Sapobah, landed there and marched to a place some four miles north of Sapobah where there were cross-roads from Benin City. There they built a stockade. On the 11th February this stockade was attacked by the Benin men from the dense bush which surrounded it, and Lieutenant-Commander Pritchard of the *Alecto* and one bluejacket were killed. After this the stockade was reinforced and strengthened. The Benin men again attacked on the 20th, but, as they did not seem to care about coming to close quarters, there were no casualties. However, the same day they attacked a column proceeding back to Sapobah, and killed one marine and wounded two others. Captain M'Gill's column returned to Warrigi on the 24th February, having previously burnt the stockade. This, of course, was after Benin City had been taken, and when the naval force was leaving the country.

The men forming the Gwatto column, under

Captain O'Callaghan, came from the *Philomel*, *Barrosa*, and *Widgeon*. On the 10th February Captain O'Callaghan burnt Gilli-Gilli, the frontier Benin City village on that side, and then proceeded on to Gwatto. After searching the bush with volleys and some rounds from a quick-firing gun, Captain O'Callaghan landed with a force of about eighty men. While they were engaged in burning the town they were attacked by a strong force of Benin men, who fought most pluckily from the bush for nearly an hour, although a number of them were seen to fall. Then they had had about enough of it, and retired. Captain O'Callaghan having blown up two big houses with gun-cotton and burnt the remainder of the town, then retired to his boats at the water-side without being attacked again. None of the force were killed, but Lieutenant - Commander Hunt of the *Widgeon* and two bluejackets were severely wounded, whilst Captain O'Callaghan himself and some others were slightly wounded.

On the 14th February the column went back to Gilli-Gilli, where they made a zereba.

However, being reinforced, they advanced again to Gwatto once more and occupied it. For two days the Benin men attacked them from the bush, but with little success, as only three men were slightly wounded, whilst the Benis lost several, and eventually never attacked at all after the 18th. On the 25th February, a company of the Protectorate Force, under Captain Gallwey, D.S.O., arrived at Gwatto from Benin City without having been once attacked, which showed that the taking of Benin City had a great effect on the Benis. On the way down, Captain Gallwey came across the scene of the massacre of our expedition, and buried the remains of our dear comrades that he found there, reading the Funeral Service over them.[1] Captain O'Callaghan embarked his force, and left Gwatto on the 27th February.

To return to the main column: but before starting an account of the march and taking

---

[1] An iron cross is to be placed here to the memory of all those poor fellows who lost their lives in the expedition, as well as a tablet in the new church at Old Calabar.

THE PUNITIVE EXPEDITION 175

of Benin City, it may be as well to explain that this column had to fight its way through twenty-two miles of dense bush country, along a narrow uncleared path that only admitted of marching single file, and almost unceasingly attacked by an unseen enemy, who used to creep up within twenty yards of the path before firing. Add to this no water to be found on the march and the excessive heat of the country, and some idea can be conceived of the work the column had to do. Of course the Admiral, now Sir Harry Rawson, K.C.B., was in supreme command, and the Consul-General of the Protectorate, now Sir Ralph Moor, K.C.M.G., accompanied him.

The advance on Ilogbo began at daylight on the 12th February, and owing to the impossibility of using the wire suspension bridge, on account of the swamps opposite Ilogbo, the force had to be conveyed by water. Though others came up later, there was only one steam-launch at Ilogbo at the commencement of the attack, which towed two surf-boats and some canoes. This was worked by that indefatigable officer Captain Child, R.N., Superintendent of the Marine Department of the Protectorate. Owing to these circumstances only a comparatively small number of men could be taken to Ilogbo at one time, and Captain Child and his launch were at work almost continuously for two days. The first detachment to start were one company of bluejackets and two companies of the Protectorate troops, under Colonel Bruce Hamilton, who commanded the advance-guard the whole way to Benin City. As soon as this detachment landed they were at once attacked by the Benis from the bush, and Captain Koe of the Protectorate Force was severely wounded, and Lieutenant Daniels, the native officer, and one private of the Force slightly wounded. As the successive detachments arrived, Colonel Hamilton pushed on, driving the enemy back, and soon occupied the Benin village of Ilogbo, which, as usual, was some distance away from the landing-place, about one thousand yards.

The 13th February was occupied in getting over the whole of the column, with its supplies

THE PUNITIVE EXPEDITION 177

and water. The advance-guard started off again at daybreak on the 14th, and after proceeding some distance, met with a strong resistance from the enemy until they reached a place where there were cross-roads, and where the enemy had apparently made their main camp. This day the Protectorate Force had one company sergeant-major and two privates severely wounded.

From Ilogbo as far as a place called Agagi, the enemy had cut a path in the bush parallel to the main path, to be used as an ambush path. They evidently were under the impression that our force would get no farther than Agagi, as the ambush path ceased there. This ambush path was an excellent thing for our Force, as it enabled two columns to proceed at the same time, and only necessitated the guarding of one flank by each column.

On the 15th February the advance-guard did not start till noon, but soon after starting they were again attacked from both sides, the attack gradually extending the whole length of the column. This went on till they reached the enemy's camp at Agagi village soon after three o'clock p.m. Here the Force had another private killed, and some of the scouts and carriers were wounded. It had been expected that some water would be found at Agagi, but all the wells were found to be dry, so now every drop of water had to be brought up from Ilogbo, some ten miles away. In consequence of this the Admiral decided to leave the Second Division of the Naval Brigade at Cross Roads Camp, while he with the advance-guard and First Division of the Naval Brigade made a dash on Benin City.

This flying column were to take with them the necessary ammunition, four days' provisions and three days' water (at the rate of two quarts for each officer or man and one quart for each carrier per day),—a terribly small quantity considering the work to be done and the excessive heat. However, it was all that could be allowed.

The advance-guard halted at Agagi on the 16th February, which place the Admiral with the Consul-General and First Division Naval

Brigade reached on the afternoon of that date. This flying column started again at daybreak on the 17th, and only reached another village called Awoko, seven miles off, about two o'clock p,m., having had a running fight nearly all the way and taken *en route* three camps of the enemy and one village. Luckily the casualties this day were small; one scout killed, one scout and one carrier severely wounded (the carrier died next day), and one bluejacket slightly wounded.

On the 18th February the column started for its final dash on Benin City, now only eight miles off. As soon as the advance-guard started they were met with a heavy fire from the back, and this continued more or less the whole day. About 10.30 a.m., Chief Petty Officer Ansell of the Navy was shot through the head from a distance about six yards off, and killed at once. About 1. p.m. the column came across a stockade which commanded a narrow causeway with a deep ravine on each side and had a few guns in it. This stockade was immediately taken and blown up with gun-cotton. About three hundred yards farther on a small village was reached, and as Benin City was reported as being near, some shells from the seven-pounders and rockets were fired in the direction the city was supposed to be. So good was the direction that next day some of the rocket-heads and the effects of the explosion of the shells were found in the city close to the King's Compound. I was also told by an officer who was present that it was reported that the King and his Juju men had actually remained in Benin City up to this time, but that a rocket coming fairly near them made them decide to quit. And quit they did, worse luck.

About one and a half miles from Benin City the column had their first experience of the sights of Benin City, for they came across two human sacrifices in the path, made most probably as Juju to stop the white men from entering the city. The wretched beings had had their arms tied behind their backs, their mouths gagged with pieces of stick, and had then been cut down and across their chests and

THE PUNITIVE EXPEDITION 181

stomachs, so that their entrails were hanging out.

Some distance after this the bush path opened up into a broad road leading to the city, which was only about a thousand yards away now. Here the enemy made a determined stand, and here for the first time were any of them seen—a party of them actually trying to charge the head of the column as it arrived at the open broad road. On arriving at the broad road the advance-guard, consisting of the Protectorate Force, bluejackets from the *St. George*, and the marine battalion, formed into square. As the square advanced it was met with a tremendously hot fire from both sides, and it was during this time that poor Captain Byrne, R.M.L.I., who only reached England to die from the effect of his wounds, was hit badly. Here also Dr. Fyfe, R.N., who had been attending to Captain Byrne, was killed, also several marines.

The enemy took every advantage of their cover from the bush, and some of them actually climbed trees to enable them to get a better chance of firing at the column. However, some of the officers of the Force made capital "rook-shooting," and killed several of the enemy in the trees. The enemy also had several old cannon firing from the direction of what was afterwards found to be the King's house. Two hundred yards from the city the column broke into a cheer and charged; the enemy fled, and Benin City was taken about two o'clock p.m. After six days' hard marching and fighting in the most extreme heat the men were naturally much exhausted.

The King's Compound was occupied by the troops for the night, and the rearguard, which had been left on the bush path, was brought up. Water was also issued to the men, leaving only one quart per man as a reserve. The casualties this day had been very heavy. Dr. Fyfe, R.N., Chief Petty Officer Ansell, R.N., and two marines had been killed; Captain Byrne, R.M.L.I., eight of the Naval Brigade and marines, three of the Protectorate Force, one scout, one native interpreter, and six

THE PUNITIVE EXPEDITION 183

carriers seriously wounded, and six of the Naval Brigade slightly wounded. I believe, also, that some of the officers were slightly wounded, but being only hit by pellets, did not return themselves as so. Major Searle of the Protectorate Force also had a narrow escape, as he twice got bullets through his helmet while working the Force seven-pounders.

On the 19th February two-thirds of the column with all the carriers were sent off to get water. They found the Ikpoba Creek (called the Ilogi Creek farther down) some two miles off, from which a plentiful supply was obtained. In fact, it was from this Creek the inhabitants of Benin City used to get all their water. Nearly all the boxes and stores of our unfortunate expedition were found almost intact in the King's Palace, but unluckily were all burned by a fire which broke out on the 21st February and burned most of the town. In this fire the house used for a hospital was burned, but, thanks to the promptitude of Captain Campbell, R.N., all the wounded and sick were got out safely.

Many of the officers of the expedition lost all their kits in this fire.

The Naval Brigade was to have left Benin for their ships on the 20th February, but as the Protectorate Force, who were to remain in Benin, were short of ammunition and stores, Admiral Rawson decided to remain till the 22nd. The whole Force was engaged for the remainder of the 19th, 20th, and 21st February, in clearing the town as much as possible, making a defensible camp for the Protectorate Force, and destroying chiefs' houses, sacrificial and crucifixion trees, and the whole of the Juju houses.

On the 19th February three of the Jakri carriers of our ill-fated expedition came in from the bush terribly mutilated. They reported that as our troops approached the city all the other wretched carriers of our expedition who had been brought there alive were at once killed, but that no white men had been brought there. All had been killed at the massacre. One of poor Mr. Gordon's boys was also found alive at the bottom of one

THE PUNITIVE EXPEDITION 185

of the deep pits amongst a lot of dead bodies. Six Accra men from the Gold Coast also came in from the bush heavily ironed. They had been captured while they were collecting rubber in the Mahin Country to the north of Benin City.

On the 21st February a carrier column, escorted by men of the Naval Brigade, arrived with stores and ammunition. The whole of the Naval Brigade left Benin City on the 22nd February, and arrived at Warrigi on the 24th, meeting with no more opposition; the flanking columns also returned soon afterwards, and the whole embarked on their ships on the 27th. This ended the Punitive Expedition. Though they did not suffer much at the time, one regrets extremely to hear that the Naval Brigade suffered badly from fever and malaria afterwards, the Cape Squadron having a very heavy sick-list from these causes, including the Admiral.

I suppose some short description of the horrors of Benin City must be given, though they are almost too dreadful to be described.

Benin City was a large rambling town divided by a broad avenue, on the south side of which were the King's and big Chiefs' Compounds, and on the north those of the lesser Chiefs and people. All these houses were built of red mud and thatched with palm leaves, part of the King's own house and the Palaver House having iron roofs.

In the King's part of the town were his own house and those of his own people, the Palaver House, Juju houses, and their Compounds, together with several old ruined houses where former kings and chiefs were supposed to be buried.

Close to the King's house were seven large Juju Compounds, each two to three acres in extent, in which most of the sacrifices were performed, and in which the people used to sit while the priest performed the sacrifices. These were large grassy enclosures, surrounded by mud walls. At one end of each, under a roof, were the sacrificial altars, on which were placed the gods—carved ivory tusks, standing upright, on hideous bronze heads. In front

THE PUNITIVE EXPEDITION 187

of each ivory god was a small earthen mound on which the wretched victim's forehead was placed. On the altars were several rudely-carved maces for killing the unfortunate victims. When the expedition took Benin City they found these altars covered with streams of dried human blood, the stench of which was too awful, the whole grass portion of the Compounds simply reeking with it.

In the corners of these Compounds huge pits, 40 to 50 feet deep, were found filled with human bodies, dead and dying, and a few wretched captives were rescued alive.

The Palaver House, which was about 100 feet long and about 50 or 60 feet broad, had an iron roof over the side walls but was open to the air in the middle. The doors were covered with embossed brass. On the roof on one side was a huge bronze snake with a large head, and in the centre of the yard a bronze crocodile's head. The King's house was much the same. Amongst its decorations were several square patches of glass let into the beams over the King's bed.

Outside, in the open space, the state of things was almost more frightful than in the Juju Compounds — everywhere sacrificial trees on which were the corpses of the latest victims— everywhere, on each path, were newly-sacrificed corpses. On the principal sacrificial tree facing the main gate of the King's Compound there were two crucified bodies, at the foot of the tree seventeen newly-decapitated bodies, and forty-three more in various stages of decomposition. On another tree a wretched woman was found crucified, while at its foot were four more decapitated bodies. To the westward of the King's house was a large open space, about 300 yards in length, simply covered with the remains of some hundreds of human sacrifices in all stages of decomposition. The same sights were met with all over the city. Such was the state of Benin City, well named the City of Blood, on the 18th January 1897. Such had been the state of the city for years, and it was by trying to see if he couldn't put a stop to such a state of things by peaceful measures, first of all, that poor Phillips and all our dear comrades lost their lives.

In conclusion, I should like to quote an extract from a letter of a comrade of the late Mr. Phillips:—" It was the disaster which befell, on 4th January, the ill-fated pacific mission, headed by Mr. Phillips, which led to the despatch of an armed expedition under Admiral Rawson, the members of which displaying gallantry and endurance beyond all praise, successfully accomplished its object and drove the monster from his throne and country.

" The loss which the British nation has sustained during the last sixty years, through the deaths of so many brave soldiers, bluejackets, and civilians in the glorious work of rescuing the native races in West Africa from the horrors of human sacrifice, cannibalism, and the tortures of fetish worship, must ever be a matter of deep regret and sadness to all; but it cannot fail to make us proud of our countrymen who have nobly and courageously done their duty with the greatest enthusiasm, undergoing hardship and privation inseparable from the trying climate of the West African Coast, and exhibiting in their conduct an entire disregard of personal danger."

THE END

www.ingramcontent.com/pod-product-compliance
Lightning Source LLC
Chambersburg PA
CBHW032228230426
43666CB00033B/1644